Sharron -
May you always
know God is fighting
for your finish!
In Christ's love,
Joe Mason

FIGHTING FOR THE FINISH

Fighting for the Finish

One Extraordinary Year

in One Ordinary Woman's Life

Jill Dorsey Mansor

Published by Fruitbearer Publishing, LLC
P.O. Box 777 • Georgetown, DE 19947
302.856.6649 • FAX 302.856.7742
fruitbearer.com • info@fruitbearer.com

Cover design by Ana Tourian
Content editing by Nancy Rue
Copy edit by Fran D. Lowe

Disclaimer

Some names and identifying details have been changed
in this memoir to protect the privacy of individuals.

Printed in the United States of America

Acknowledgements

—~~~—

I would not have made the decision to accept Jesus Christ if Pastor Don Polk had not led me in the salvation prayer for redemption on Friday, September 1, 1995, at 7:00 a.m. Pastor Don, I am forever grateful to you and your willingness to *always be ready to share the gospel of peace.*

I would also like to thank my faithful friends, Sharon Constantine and Susan Shute. They helped me through a treacherous period in my life and gave me a foundation so that I could fly and soar with my Lord and Savior, Jesus Christ.

I will be forever indebted to my faithful encourager, my husband, Dan. He makes me feel as if I can do anything, and in knowing him, I have been encouraged to reach for more goals than at any other time in my life.

My parents have always encouraged me to take chances, and, as my mother loves to say, "What do you have to lose?" This has been my motto, which has essentially encouraged me to sometimes do what I think, and feel is impossible.

To all who read this book, I pray that you too may come to know the living and loving Jesus Christ. May you come to believe that "He who is in you is greater than he who is in the world."

———♦———

Chapter 1

—∿∿—

It was happening again. This time it came in the form of a frantic bee buzzing around me searching for a weakness. I swung my arms like a world-class baseball player trying to bat it away, but it landed under my armpit and planted its stinger in my body. As the bee tore away, reeling in death, I knew it was an attack launched by the devil himself. Angrily pulsating, a red, swollen welt formed, and the pain vibrated and throbbed through my body. It was just one more sign that made me feel "something" hated me here.

What was I doing here? As a single woman, I was often asked by my friends to stay at their homes while they enjoyed their vacations. It was a welcome change from going to bars looking for Mr. Right, which so far hadn't worked out for me anyway.

"Here" was a home—a term I use loosely because it was actually a mansion of over six thousand square feet—that stood on over eighty acres of prime real estate near a quaint little town in southern New Jersey. Although it was gorgeous at the time, it had lain in disrepair for many decades before it was bought by my friend, Beth, and her family.

I first learned about the house when Beth decided to buy it and restore it to its once grand state. In anticipation of Beth's acquisition of the property, I drove out to see it one cold winter day. The wind whistled through the broken windows, and the door banged and thumped. A dead tree behind the house scratched its bare branches across the roof, which only added to its eerie character. The floors were dry rotted, and you could see that the once grand entrance was littered with debris from whomever had broken into the house. The house looked menacing, and it made me feel very uncomfortable.

I loved the old age of the house, though, with its winding staircase, which I could imagine some wonderful woman dressed in a long gown slowly gliding down to meet her waiting friends and family. The mansion was built for entertaining, featuring grand rooms, twenty-foot ceilings, hardwood floors, and crown moldings of etched motifs and elaborate patterns which revealed the love and design originally put into this house.

I knew that Beth would restore the home to its original splendor. She and her husband owned a company whose profits were skyrocketing into the stratosphere, so money was no object.

While they fixed up this mansion, she lived in a small six-acre farm not far from there. It was here that I originally met Beth. She was pregnant with her third child and not doing well with the pregnancy. She was looking for someone to ride her cantankerous horse while she took some time off to be a parent. My riding instructor heard about the opportunity, and she immediately thought of me. Because of my inability to purchase a horse of my own, I was very willing to exercise her horse while she was on hiatus.

This was supposed to be a vacation for *me* too. A pool, horse farm, and a gorgeous house to lounge in was an escape that I could relish.

Leaping at the opportunity, I was delighted to stay in this mansion and take care of the many horses in her barn.

But unfortunately, it wasn't turning out that way. Though it was only six in the morning on day 6, I was already exhausted because I was no longer sleeping in Beth's home at night.

I actually tried for two days, but the house made me feel very uncomfortable. Music would play without anyone turning on the stereo, chairs would move, and lights would turn on by themselves. The noises scared me the most. I would turn around quickly, sensing that someone was looking at me. There was an angry energy in the atmosphere that was unmistakable and very scary.

At first, I made excuses for the home and these idiosyncrasies. I reasoned that maybe the music from the stereo and the lights were on a timer and the chairs moved because of the dogs. Not only that, but Beth told me when she first bought the house, the construction workers said they felt an eerie presence there. One guy fled in the middle of a job and never came back. She herself had said she felt something dwelled in her house. The difference was that she liked it and it apparently liked her. Clearly, however, it did not like me.

It would not let me rest. What was most disconcerting was the fact that my dog, Amy, a Lab mix, would not go in the house. This was a dog that would cry as soon as I left her alone. She would walk through fire to be with me. Her life revolved around me. My dog basically confirmed what I wanted to deny—that there was danger in this house. After much coaxing, she would grudgingly come in with tail tucked and head down. Her fur rising on her back, she was fearful of what I could sense but she seemed to see.

———◠◠◠———

On day 2, I decided to call the Catholic diocese in Philadelphia. I am not a Catholic, nor is anyone in my family, but I had heard that they believed homes could be haunted. The logical solution was to call them and explain what I was experiencing. A sweet older woman picked up my call.

"All right, dearie, tell me what is happening at this house you are watching?" Her sweet grandmotherly voice was soothing.

"Um . . . lights go on without anyone being in the room. I hear noises, like humming, bumping, screeching, and thumping. Chairs move, and my dog, a Lab mix, won't even come into the house, which is weird because this dog would follow me if I walked into fire. I don't know—I'm just scared." I blurted that last part out.

"Hmm, that sounds like there may be some activity there. How old is the house?" she asked.

"Old, like hundreds of years old. It was abandoned for many years, and then my friend bought it and fixed it up. She hired me to stay here, but I'm too scared. Do you think I'm in danger?"

"Dearie, I think you shouldn't stay there. Just do what you must do to take care of it, but I think you shouldn't put yourself in danger," she answered.

"Thank you for your time; I really appreciate it," I said. Echoing through my head was her voice telling me not to put myself in danger.

While Beth was gone, my responsibilities included feeding the horses, teaching riding lessons, cleaning the barn, and taking care of this beautiful home. My heart was torn. I wanted to do all of that and more, but, again, I could not stay at her home at night. So, I decided to compromise and spend the nights at my own home in Delaware. I would come early in the morning and then leave around nine or ten at night. Every day I would set the home alarm and take her gigantic black Doberman Pinscher, Alfred, to my house to share my bed with Amy and me. I wanted Beth to enjoy her vacation, so I didn't bother her with any of my suspicions that anything was amiss at her home.

The problem was that now, on day 6, it became clear the disturbing events weren't happening just at night. The bee attack happened while the sun was shining brightly over the farm. A feeling of dread crept deeper and deeper into my mind and heart. Tiny pinpricks of fear clamored as they danced up my back and onto my neck, breaking into a crescendo at the crown of my head.

I drove to the barn on a separate driveway from the house. It wound through a deep forest across a small bridge and over a babbling brook. The barn, along with the covered indoor arena that allowed riders to exercise their horses no matter the weather, sat upon a hill. Today they sat glistening in the sunlight like a diamond.

This horse farm was unlike many farms in the area. There were several riding rings, an indoor riding arena, outdoor cross-country course, and a stadium jumping arena. The heated barn came complete with a vacuum to groom the horses, and it also boasted a wash stall with hot and cold water to ensure that each horse got a royal bath. The tack room was heated in the winter and air-conditioned in the summer. Comfortable over-stuffed couches and chairs adorned the tack room too. Riders often gathered together there to share stories about their horses, and a crowd of boarders and lesson students could also be found relaxing in this room.

It was here that I taught riding lessons, a position I held with great regard because Beth had entrusted me to begin the horseback riding program at her grand farm. I was proud to be a part of this beautiful farm with its many amenities for the horses as well as the riders.

As I walked into the barn, the horses whinnied in excitement for their feed. I usually called to them by name, but after my run-in with the bee, I was frankly in no mood to be cheery. I went into the feed room and turned on the lights. They flickered on and off—something they had never done before—and it just aggravated me even more. Frustrated and irritated, I found myself getting impatient. This was another indication that something *was* here, and it had chosen to harass and hound my every step.

Hearing tires on the gravel road to the barn, I glanced out the window to see my friend, Sharon, driving up to the barn. I had met Sharon at the high school where I was working in the fall of 1990. She was the school nurse, and I taught special education. We had similar personalities in that we were both nurturing and caring. We loved the students, and we would mutually come to the same conclusions while helping many of our most difficult charges.

When she discovered her husband no longer wanted to be married, she was devastated, but she started attending a small country church where she said she found strength and peace by getting to know God. Frequently, she would share the pastor's lessons and teachings with me. I listened halfheartedly because, to be truthful, I did not really believe in God. She was definitely not one of the friends I went bar-hopping with.

As I greeted her at the barn door, I said, "Look at this," instead of offering my usual hello. I raised my arm and pointed to the now red lump that had grown to the size of a golf ball under my arm.

"What happened?" she said, squinting to inspect it.

"I was attacked this morning. And it wasn't just accidental—that bee came straight at me like something told it to."

As if in perfect unison with this account, the lights flickered and sputtered. We were not alone. Shuddering, I could see that Sharon was shaking too. I fought the urge to flee, but my nerves needed release, so I started to laugh—high and shrill like a ten-year-old. Sharon joined me.

Sharon was the only one with whom I could share any of these scary experiences. I trusted her because she was a born-again Christian and believed in the existence of supernatural happenings, just like I did. If I'd told any of my other friends or my boyfriend, they would have thought I'd gone insane.

Besides, it wasn't like I had a choice. I'd been there only a day when Sharon stopped by with some pizza and cool watermelon chillers she purchased from a produce stand.

I was surprised that she stopped by unannounced yet touched that she was thinking of me. We sat on the couch with the steaming pizza in front of us and a good movie, *Black Beauty*, in the VCR. We sat back with the pizza in our hands and began to watch the movie, when it began fast-forwarding on its own. At first, we thought we had accidentally touched the remote control, but it was laying on the table. We both looked at each other and began to giggle nervously. Then it resumed the normal play speed.

We sat back again, relaxing and enjoying the tasty pizza. Suddenly, the volume dropped to zero, so we could not hear the movie at all. We both scrambled for the remote control, but it was to no avail. Regardless of how hard we pushed the button, we could not get the volume to go up. In frustration, we turned off the VCR, and I related what had been happening there. She was initially shocked but then confessed that she felt a weird presence there too.

The next day she started coming to help with the feeding—and share my fears. Upon hearing our laughter now, the horses understood that their food would be coming soon, and their neighs and whinnies swelled to a cacophony of noise. As if snapped back to our primary purpose at that moment, we looked at each other and then began preparing their feed and hay.

"Let's each load up a cart," I said. "You take that end of the barn, and I'll take this one."

Within a few minutes, the horses were happily slurping and chomping on their feed. Sharon had involuntarily become a horsewoman, and I appreciated her willingness to help me. The horses' halter rings clanged in time with their greedy mouths, which made a harmonious song I would never tire of hearing.

"All this feeding is making me hungry," Sharon said. "Have you had breakfast?"

"I didn't have time."

Sharon nodded. She was the only person I'd told that I was making the trek home every night and leaving at the crack of dawn to get back here.

In the feed room, I grabbed the empty feed barrel for a seat and Sharon grabbed a stool, but she didn't sit right away. She laid out an elaborate breakfast, and I admired her ability to always be so giving and thoughtful. She knew that I probably had not eaten, so she made time to stop on her way to the barn to get us freshly baked croissants with strawberry jam and small Styrofoam cups of steaming black coffee. It was all delicious, and it gave me something to think about besides all the things that were freaking me out.

"I've already eaten two of these," I said as I started to pick up another croissant. I paused when the phone rang. It echoed throughout the barn, interrupting the melodious sounds of content horses eating their breakfast.

I rocketed off the barrel and ran to the other end of the barn to the office. After twisting the doorknob and realizing that it was locked, I grabbed the key above the door jamb and hastily unlocked the door. Practically leaping across the desk, I grabbed the phone. I held it to my ear and began to speak when I heard the dial tone on the other end. Thinking it strange, I ran to the feed room, where Sharon was cleaning up the remains of our breakfast and feeding the barn cats.

"Sharon," I said, "it was weird. As soon as I picked up the phone, all I heard was a dial tone. You know, that 'nnnnnnnnnnnnn' sound?"

"That *is* weird," she said looking at the clock. "It's only 6:30 in the morning. Who do you think was calling?" The cute little calico kitten jumped into her lap, and she fed it a tiny piece of her croissant.

"I don't know. I hope it wasn't Beth," I said, knowing I tend to think the worst. I didn't want Beth to know that I wasn't staying at her house at night.

We began our routine of letting the horses out one at a time into their designated pastures. I started at one end and Sharon at the other. I took out the boarding horses, and Sharon led out the docile lesson ones. At the end was a beautiful black Thoroughbred named Thunder. He was over seventeen hands high, and his presence struck awe in all who met him. I reached up to attach the lead line to his leather halter and opened the door wide to get him to his pasture twenty feet away.

As soon as my foot graced the threshold, the phone rang.

I pushed Thunder back into his stall, and he unhappily shook his head at me. I ran as fast as I could to the office. I pushed the door open so hard that it knocked into the door stop and all the papers on the desk flew off. I was determined to get this call. But again, all I heard was the "nnnnnnnnnnn" sound of a disconnected line. I sat on top of the desk, puzzled. It was now 6:42, and there had already been two calls. Someone must need me.

I started to gather the papers and neatly place them on the desk. I waited for a few minutes until I heard Thunder's whinny for me to come back to reality and set him free. I left the office door open so there would be nothing but a clear shot from the stalls to the phone.

I snapped the lead on Thunder once again. As soon as my foot hit the cool concrete of the aisle, the phone blared out again, piercing the air. I pushed the big black Thoroughbred back into the stall again. This time, he jerked around and tried to pull me back into the aisle. He pinned his ears and made a menacing face as if he meant to harm me if I didn't let him go. I insisted and shut the stall door just in time as his teeth bore down at me.

The feet of a gazelle could not have run faster than mine, and I slid across the desk like a baseball player rounding for home. But it was all to no avail. As I reached for the phone, all I heard was that same "nnnnnnnnnnn" sound. I slammed the receiver back into its cradle. This time I pulled the thing off the desk. As the phone sat precariously in the aisle, it would be easier for me to reach should it ring again.

I walked back to Thunder and told him that I was sorry. He paced and pranced in the stall, arching his neck, each muscle rippling in the sunlight. He did not trust me, and I couldn't blame the big fellow. I opened the door and started to walk him outside into the crisp, beautiful morning as he pulled me in anticipation of having a great gallop around the field.

As soon as I let him off the lead, he reared and struck the air with purpose. When he landed, the sound of thunder could be heard from his mighty hooves. Then he sprang into a full gallop, completing five large bucks. He was beautiful and majestic. Glancing over his shoulder, he paused to see if I was watching his grandiose show of power and might, and then he shook his head as if he knew I was admiring his antics.

Suddenly, I heard the faint ringing of the barn phone. I sprang into action, running like a world-class sprinter. In record time, which even Steve Prefontaine, the world's greatest runner, would have had a hard time beating, I jumped across the aisle and impressively reached for the phone. Breathlessly, I breathed into the receiver and heard the aggravating "nnnnnnnnnn."

I screamed as loud as I could, "I hate this haunted, weird, demonic place! I can't take it anymore! I want out of here!"

After voicing what I had repressed over the past few days, the truth of it caught me off guard. I was in a place of uncertainty and strife where I was not in control, and its unfamiliarity made me angry. There was no way I could explain, rationalize, work through, or find a solution to help me with this force that was unseen and unnamed.

I composed myself and started to let the last horse out, a beautiful palomino quarter horse named Que. He was my favorite horse at the farm. With his quirky personality, he was always full of mischief. His favorite treat was honey buns, and he loved to torture me by pulling on my clothing looking for the elusive goodie that I would hide in a side pocket. He was quite a handful to lead because he used his lips to tickle me. I spoiled him terribly. He was a great lesson horse and one of the favorite mounts for my students to ride. He always made me laugh, and I needed that now.

The sun glimmered in the sky, and I heard the faint sound of a faraway owl. I could also hear the barn phone ringing. I knew I would never be able to reach it, so I took my time leading Que out to his paddock. I held up the honey bun and he greedily ate it. Then he licked my hands, and I kissed his beautiful, dignified face. I let him graze on the sweet grass outside of the barn and buried my head in his strong neck. His sweet aroma gave me comfort, and I desired that feeling more than ever. He pulled his head up as if to reassure me, and I scratched him under his chin.

I reluctantly put him out and secured his gate with two chains. He was a real Houdini and could undo any lock with those infamous lips of his. He stood watching me.

"No, Que," I said. "There will be no loose horses on my watch." I reluctantly left him, not knowing what I would face once I got back to the barn.

As I rounded the entrance to the barn, I could hear the phone ringing again. Sharon met me in the barn office and sat on the sofa across from the desk. I could tell she wanted to say something, but there was nothing to say. I was slowly losing all dignity and control over myself. I placed my head in my hands and then wiped my eyes.

"I can't take this anymore," I said, fighting back tears. "This is destroying me. The truth is, I'm scared. I can't fight this by myself. I'm ill-equipped."

Sharon said nothing, but her face said it all. She knew that there was *something* here, a presence that was menacing and looming in every room and stall. This ominous and threatening spirit hung over us like a dank odor. It intimidated us and convinced us that we were at its mercy. The jail sentence had been handed out, and what we were guilty of we did not know or understand.

The phone rang again. This time I did not hold it to my ear; instead, I picked it up and slammed it down. Anger recoiled like a snake and lifted its ugly head from the depths of my soul. I gritted my teeth and grunted. Sharon sat with a look of horror on her face. We were both terrified.

Abruptly, Sharon said, "I have an idea. Let me call my pastor. His name is Don, and he's wonderful. I told him about you last night, and I explained what has been happening here. He told me to tell you that you should call him."

"No, Sharon," I said. "I don't want to talk to a pastor. What is *he* going to do?" I was incredulous. To me, pastors were weak people with stiff personalities. Talking to a pastor, I thought, would be a waste of my time.

The phone rang again. I guess this was the theme for today: a ringing phone to drive me crazy. I shook my head as tears welled in my eyes. As I accidentally hit the bump that was now the size of a softball under my arm, I winced in pain, recalling the first assault of the day.

Sharon picked up the phone while I busied myself with straightening the papers on the desk. I knew who she was calling. I glanced at the wall clock. It was barely seven in the morning.

"Pastor Don," she said, "I'm sorry to call you this early, but it seems that things are out of control here and I think Jill needs to talk to you. Remember, she's the girl who's staying at her friend's farm while the family is on vacation? . . . . Yes, it's starting again, but it has never happened this early or so intensely before now. She was stung by a bee, and the phone has been ringing incessantly with no one on the line . . . . Would you like to talk to her?" She paused and held the phone at arm's length, and with her free arm, she waved frantically like she was holding the keys of hope for those in despair.

I vehemently shook my head and placed my arms across my chest. I continued with my business of organizing the papers until she held the phone up to my face, and then she did the unthinkable. She walked away, forcing me to pick it up.

I held the phone up to my ear. Choked with frustration, my voice came out cracked and weak as I uttered, "Hello."

"Is this Jill?" His gentle voice was calmly reassuring. I just wasn't sure I could trust it.

"Yes, I understand that Sharon told you about me and what we're experiencing here," I said.

His calm voice evoked a feeling of peace, and I longed for it like nothing else before. I was like a weary traveler yearning for rest, and his voice was a soft, downy pillow that was oddly comforting to my soul. This might be the strangest happening yet: five minutes ago, I was resisting him like one of the horses would do. Yet now, I was all ears.

"Yes, Sharon did tell me about you and where you're staying. I actually know the place. If I'm correct, it's one of the oldest historic sites in New Jersey. What exactly are you experiencing there?"

He wanted to know every detail. Like a faucet, I turned on the spigots full blast and spilled out the whole story—the music that blared out of unseen speakers in the house, the TV that changed channels and the rise and fall of the volume without any button being touched, the chair that scraped across the wooden floor even though no one was near it, the chandelier that was only partially lit, and the screaming fight I heard on the balcony outside the bedroom I was staying in the first night. I told him about the ferocious thunderstorm that night, which rumbled and roared while spitting out bolts of lightning as if it were a battle between good and evil. I told him about the banging and thumping pervading the house—no matter how hard I searched, I could never find the source. I shared how I turned the lights off, but as soon as I got to the balcony, every single light in the house came on. I told him about the flickering barn lights, the red welt under my arm, and the persistent phone ringing with a dead line as soon as I answered.

I told him about my faithful dog that would whimper and refuse to step foot in certain rooms. At times her fur would stand up around her neck, and she would snarl as if she were protecting me. She would stare and follow an invisible force that seemed to float above her.

I realized I had been recalling these weird happenings without taking a breath. My heart was pounding as I involuntarily paced nervously in the small office.

Pointedly, I asked, "Am I in danger?"

He took a deep breath and said, "Yes, I do believe you are. Accept Jesus as your personal Savior. He is the only one who has the power to break the stronghold of these demons. Once you ask Jesus into your heart, His blood will cover your sins and you will be His. No one will be able to mess with you. You will have the power to overcome these demonic forces that are . . . quite obviously harassing you. Now, would you like to accept Jesus as your personal Savior?"

He had given a name to these forces: demons. I had watched scary movies about supernatural forces, but I did not think that they existed. I was frightened and confused. Why were they harassing me?

All I could think of was how much I disliked Christians. They always seemed so judgmental and condemning. Pastor Don was just the opposite, however. He had a soft, soothing voice, and it seemed that he had a lot of experience with people who were in trouble or frightened. He was calming me by validating these frightening occurrences. And most important, he held out a solution. He talked about Jesus' blood and the cleansing of sins. However, I felt I did not fit in with the other sinners of the world. I reasoned that I was a good person and my sins were not all that bad.

He continued to talk about the blood of Christ and that all people are sinners and need the Savior. I halfheartedly listened as he spoke, since I had always believed that Christians were crazy, and I didn't want to be one of them. I could not comprehend powers I could not see, yet I seemed to be in the midst of them. It seemed the only thing I was certain about was that I did not want to be a born-again Christian. I liked my life the way it was, and I was certain that it would go back to normal once I left this place. All I needed to do was leave this disturbed house and farm, and I reasoned that would be happening in precisely two short days, sixteen hours and thirty minutes.

"No thanks," I said emphatically.

No sooner had I said those words than the phone started to ring while I was on it. I held it away from my ear and stared quizzically at it. Sharon quickly came back into the office. I motioned to her that I was still speaking with Pastor Don but the phone was ringing again. This was impossible because there was no other line. How could the phone be ringing while I was on it?

My mind raced ahead. *Would I be in this condition forever? Would I be harassed by demons for the rest of my life? Surely this was supernatural and demonic.*

"If I accept Jesus as my personal Savior, will this stop?" I asked him, as the unremitting ringing of the phone interrupted my thoughts and I began losing my concentration. What I really wanted at that moment was rest and, more important, peace. I knew this pastor had the answer for me.

"I don't know," Pastor Don replied. "What I do know is that if you accept Jesus, you will have the power to come against these demonic forces because He will be in you. Therefore, you will also have His power." He paused, but only for a second. "Jill, whether you realize this or not, you're in a dangerous place. It's not only dangerous for you physically but spiritually as well. I won't be able to help you, and Sharon won't be able to help you. Jesus is the only one who can help you now."

He said this so forcefully that I was frightened. I knew deep in my heart, however, that what he was saying was the truth.

The phone continued to ring, interrupting our conversation. His words soaked into my brain. I was faced with the reality that I would not be able to escape this harassment, and it pierced the core of my being. A perfect compromise arose in my mind, and I leapt at the chance to use Jesus at this time to get rid of these forces. This was a viable solution to me. Then, I believed, I could forget all about this and resume my normal life.

"Okay, how do I accept Jesus into my life?" I asked as the ringing continued.

He took a deep breath and said, "First, you need to confess that you are a sinner. Then you need to ask Him to wash you clean of your sins. Ask Him to dwell in your heart. That's all."

"But how do I accept Jesus?" The simplicity of salvation hadn't sunk in yet. There must be more to it than this.

"Why don't you just repeat this after me?" He didn't wait for me to respond but just plunged forward. "Jesus, I recognize that I am a sinner . . . ."

He paused for me to repeat after him, which I did.

"I ask that you wash me clean of my sins . . . ."

"Come dwell in my heart, Jesus . . . ."

After I said the prayer, relief and peace inundated my thoughts and permeated my being. The phone had finally stopped ringing, and I felt free. In that brief moment of prayer directed by the pastor, I knew something had happened inside of me and somehow, I was different.

I was hoping that now all of this harassment would stop, and life would become normal again. Little did I know that things would get a lot worse before they would ever get better.

⸺⟋⟋⟋⟍⟍⟍⸺

Chapter 2

Within an hour of accepting Jesus as my personal Savior, I was tested and tried. Suddenly the office and barn seemed to vibrate. I could hear a dark, dissonant humming sound throughout the building, which could only mean that the demonic forces were roaring to life so strongly, both the house and barn were coming alive with supernatural activity. It was as if they were punishing me for accepting Jesus.

Ignoring the sound, I set out to sweep the expansive barn alley. There is always comfort in the mundane, ordinary chores of a horse farm. I was often the only person who enjoyed picking out a stall or sweeping until there was not a strand of hay to be seen. I enjoyed the before and after activities of barn work because their simplicity allowed my brain to relax while my body worked.

Sharon enjoyed it too, and she would work alongside me or sit on the outside bench soaking up the sun and watching the horses' antics that graced this beautiful farm. On this day, she sat and read a book, frequently pausing to push back her hair that kept falling in her face. Then I noticed she was writing in a small spiral notebook.

"Whatcha writing about?" I asked her.

"That you accepted Christ!" With a broad smile, she raised her open hand. I knew that this simple act had a profound significance, even though I could not comprehend its meaning.

"I know—I feel different too. A weird feeling has come over me. Like an awareness. I don't know, it's just weird," I could not formulate the words that expressed what I felt, but I knew I was different somehow. My world was slightly askew, and there was a quickening in my heart every time I thought about Jesus or God.

"Jill, you are born again!" she declared. Her smile grew even broader.

"Yeah, that's what Pastor Don said." I did not know at the time what becoming a born-again Christian meant.

The crackle of pebbles against rubber tires alerted us to someone driving up the barn driveway. We both craned our necks to see who was coming to the barn this early. It was a tired-looking mini-van with dirty windows. Someone had written in its thin veil of dirt on the side of the van, "WASH ME!" The engine sputtered and finally came to rest at the top of the hill next to the feed room door.

Spilling out of the car was the Jones family—with all six of their children. The oldest, Fran, was fourteen, and the youngest was the tiny toddler, Saddie, sixteen months. Somewhere in the middle of the pack was ten-year-old Jethro, a real terror and a bit of a handful for the worn and irritated mother. Before they were even out of the car, he was nagging her to get his gorgeous BMX bike out of the back, so he could ride it while Fran was having her lesson.

Fran had been taking lessons at another farm that exchanged her barn work for a riding education. She was a decent rider and relatively new to competitive riding, yet, like a sponge soaking up water, she absorbed everything taught to her. I guess Mrs. Jones reasoned that in Jethro's case, riding his bike was not a bad trade-off for peace instead of his ever-present whining about being at a horse farm where he couldn't do anything but sit there and watch his sister.

Mrs. Jones unfastened the now screaming Saddie. Apparently, the toddler wanted to be free and run around carelessly like her older siblings. While Fran went to the barn, Jethro headed out to the space where he could pop wheelies, spin, and ride the trails with abandon. Appeasing Saddie, Mrs. Jones allowed her to walk ahead, and the little girl focused on the sleeping barn cat huddled on top a bale of hay. But just as she held out her stubby little arms, ready to grasp the sleeping victim, the cat launched like a rocket-propelled missile out of harm's way and into the woods. The crying began again, so Mrs. Jones picked Saddie up and tried to console her, but she cried even louder.

I came out of the stall with pitchfork in hand and went over to her.

"Does Saddie want to feed Que?" I asked.

"Yesssss!" the little girl exclaimed through her tears.

"Yes, what?" her mother corrected her.

"Yes, please!" Her face brightened as I held out the Holy Grail of all treats known to horses—a sticky bun.

Mrs. Jones smiled and thanked me with a sigh of relief. Saddie grabbed my hand, and we walked to the field where Que was resting under the cool shade of a huge oak tree.

"Que, Que, Que!" Saddie screamed.

Que trotted over after seeing and hearing the glistening cellophane wrapper of a sticky bun. He perched his head low as I carefully unwrapped the sticky bun and placed it in a small rubber pail that we used to feed the horses treats.

Saddie held out the treat, and Que, always mindful of his manners, delicately picked it up with his lips and swallowed it in a gulp. I helped her put the bowl down and outside the fence. Otherwise, Que would happily hold this bowl in his mouth all day in hopes that someone would give him a treat. He was quite the jokester at the farm, and many hours of laughter were a result of something Que was doing with his lips.

"More?" Saddie asked, motioning for me to give her another sticky bun.

"No more, Saddie. Que will get sick if we give him more than one sticky bun," I said when she started to place her tiny hand in mine.

She knew the rules: No one was allowed near the horses unless they were supervised. I was a real stickler for safety. Being around horses for twenty-five years had taught me valuable lessons in being cautious and respectful around even of the most docile of horses.

We walked back into the barn, and the cute calico kitten sidled up to my leg. I reached down and grabbed it so that Saddie could finally pet a kitten. Tenderly she stroked the small cat, and it began to purr. Saddie squealed with delight and tried to pick it up, but I shook my head in disapproval. She sat down on the bale of hay, and I put the tiny kitten in her lap. Her mother smiled with delight and sighed in relief that her daughter was finally happy.

Mrs. Jones was a no-nonsense type of woman. Rarely did I ever hear a pleasantry or compliment uttered to any of her children. Because she was so busy, she would usually drop Fran off early on Saturday morning and pick her up as I was ready to leave around five o'clock in the afternoon. Many times, I fed Fran a part of my sandwich or bought one for her. She became a farm fixture and one whom I could count on to help me with lessons, tacking up a horse, or helping a student with a question.

Only once during the past year of teaching did her mother even stay and watch a lesson, and sadly at Fran's first show, she came one minute too late to see her daughter compete. My heart broke for her because I knew she wanted her mother to see her ride. Although a lousy substitute for a mother, I was always encouraging and complimentary. I made sure to give her something every Saturday for all her help, such as treats for her horse, a halter my horse grew out of, a saddle blanket I no longer needed, or a name plate for her horse's stall.

Mrs. Jones cocked her hip and held a tense hand out to me. She seemed very upset.

"Jill, my daughter needs help with her horse. Can you ride him sometime today?" she asked. The veins stood out in her neck, and Fran looked down at the ground, one boot on top of the other. Their old trainer had encouraged their barely-scraping-by family to get a free horse from the local racetrack. Although the horse was gorgeous, he had a nasty temperament, and it was not uncommon for him to try to bite, kick, buck, or rear at will. The horse was too much for the young girl, and now they were here at the most premier farm in all southern New Jersey, hoping for a miracle.

"I don't know if I can do it today. I'm pretty busy. I will try to jump on if I have time," I replied. Her horse took every ounce of my ability to concentrate. Admittedly, I was off my game and a little tentative about jumping on her wild, menacing maniac of a horse.

Mrs. Jones gritted her teeth, and then it became painfully clear that Fran would not be able to ride unless one of the trainers got on her horse. Even though this girl had been thrown, bit, and kicked, as well as broken her collarbone, she loved this animal because he was her very first. Immediately, I began to backtrack in my mind and figure out when I could jump on her horse so that this precious child could ride.

"All right," I said. "I'm willing to—"

But my voice was cut off by a bloodcurdling scream. A crash followed.

I ran toward the sound, right behind Mrs. Jones, before I completely knew what it was, even though that became immediately apparent. Young Jethro was in a heap against the fence in the pasture, grabbing his knee while his bike lay beside him, front wheel still spinning.

I had almost reached him when my body involuntarily froze, and my eyes were immediately riveted to a dark pool of crimson blood about twenty yards ahead, between me and the boy. It blocked my path as I reeled backwards to get away, but my body would not move. My feet were glued to the ground as if they were stuck in cement. My eyes were transfixed, and I was unable to blink or look away from this colossal pool of blood that seemed to pulsate and throb as if it were alive. My heart pounded in fear.

I tried to blink or avert my eyes, but I was unable to. Riveted to the spot, I stared at the pool of blood, which seemed to represent everything that was evil. Then the words of Pastor Don echoed in my mind. I could hear his audible voice, which had spoken just a few minutes ago, resonate in my mind: "Only Jesus can help you—not you, not me, not Sharon—only Jesus."

"Jesus, help me!" I cried.

As soon as I said this, my eyes blinked, and a cold fear blanketed my heart. Then I felt a chill run down the back of my neck and then up my spine. The minute hairs on the back of my neck stood at attention from fear. My instinct begged me to leave, run, and hide.

I became acutely aware that this was a war of colossal proportions and consequences being waged against me. I was slowly learning that I was not equipped or prepared to fight. However, I became increasingly aware and emboldened that I had the right weapon: Jesus. He was my only hope in getting through this ordeal alive.

Sharon was now on the scene, and I could feel her agitation and concern in her body's stiffness as she crouched beside me.

"What happened?" she asked.

I couldn't speak. All I could do was shake my head. Tears started to fall from my eyes. She looked intently in my face.

"What's going on?" she repeated.

Her panicked voice registered in my mind, but when I tried to reply, I couldn't.

Then, whatever had me bound now loosened its grip, so I was able to talk.

"Sharon, it hates me," I said through gritted teeth.

She looked questioningly at me. I searched for words to describe what had happened, but there were none. Nothing was making sense. All I knew was that there was an angry force here and it was trying to destroy me. I had lost control over myself. I could not take my eyes off the blood. For the first time in my life, I was powerless.

"Sharon, I saw all this blood," I started to say. "What is so baffling is that I couldn't avert my eyes."

"Where was it?" she asked.

"Only fifteen feet away from us . . . right over there," I said, pointing to a spot of overgrown brush.

Sharon stared at the spot, trying to see anything, but it was gone. She shook her head, as if trying to get an image out of her head. She was becoming as confused and as scared as I was.

I began walking quickly toward the house, my only escape. If I went over to the boy, I would have to help. Going toward the barn meant riding a maniacal horse. Going to the house seemed to be the only logical choice. I reasoned that I was the one who needed help. Somehow, I had digest what happened, and I certainly did not need anyone to distract me. I could hear Sharon following me. My feet were carrying me swiftly, and I allowed them to take me where I had to go.

I had to feed the hamster, Gilbert, along with the two gerbils, Mickey and Minnie. I quickly deactivated the alarm and opened the door. I could hear the little gerbils spring into action on their noisy wheel. The hamster was quiet as usual, but he still scratched at his glass cage to let me know that he was expecting extra sunflower seeds. They were kept in the laundry room, and this was the first room that I let myself into. I took off my boots and began to feed the cute little critters. *What a contrast to horses*, I chuckled to myself as they fought for their food. I scratched them with my index finger, and they rolled on their backs, relishing the attention. I was immediately soothed, even if just for the moment.

Sharon quietly let herself into the house. She liked little Minnie, so she squatted down at her cage to enjoy her antics while I went into the kitchen to make some tea.

"Sharon, do you want some tea?" I called out to her.

"Sounds good! Do you think Beth has honey?" she asked.

"Uh, what do you think? Hmmm . . . six-thousand-dollar refrigerator, million-dollar home, gazillion-dollar barn, I think she probably has some honey!" I couldn't resist being a little sarcastic, and immediately I was sorry for it.

Sharon followed me into the kitchen, and we both washed our hands.

After getting out our tea cups, I plopped an Earl Grey tea bag in each one. I rummaged through the likely cabinets that would hold the elusive honey. Sharon stood behind me, marveling at all the food, spices, cookies, crackers, and beautiful hand-crafted dinnerware and mugs. She chose a gorgeous hand-painted yellow mug with bright red and blue flowers. I grabbed the refined Lenox china tea cup with its sterling silver lining. My hands were still shaking.

Then we both paused. The tea kettle, beginning its slow boil, started to whistle. I picked up the kettle from the burner to stop its wail. It was unmistakable—there was another sound. Sharon and I both looked at each other. Holding the kettle, I began to pour the boiling water into our cups.

"Sharon, do you hear that?" I asked.

We both stood still, and in that moment a low humming began to vibrate, from the third story to the basement.

"Yeah, what is that?" Her blue eyes opened wide.

"I don't know. I heard it the first time I came into this house. Hmmm, maybe it has to do with the electrical wiring in the house."

The humming began again in earnest, as if confirming our suspicions. The microscopic hairs stood erect on the back of my neck as a chill coursed through my body. I shivered.

"Sharon, what on earth is that?"

"I don't know!"

"Sharon, look at the kitchen table!" I almost screamed.

One of the kitchen chairs had moved and was sitting at an angle as if someone had just hastily gotten up. No one was at that table, and certainly no one had sat in that chair.

"What on earth is going on?" Sharon almost screamed.

"I don't know. But did you see the chair move?"

"No, did you?" she asked, her mouth forming a small O.

"No, not really. I just saw something out of the corner of my eye, and when I glanced over there, I noticed the chair had moved."

We both grabbed our mugs of tea and took long sips to comfort ourselves. Then it was as if something was compulsorily willing us to be hysterical. The humming turned into a discordance of thumping and banging that resounded throughout the house, as if it was angry that we had come into its center. The sound grew louder, so it was impossible for Sharon and me to ignore it.

Tearing into us like a knife, the phone rang.

I looked at Sharon. It rang again, but I did not want to pick it up. *Would it be a dead phone line again?* I wondered as I began to reach for it. Sharon's eyes widened with terror. Surely, she was thinking the same thing.

Touching the phone set off an electrical shock that ripped through my body with such force that I dropped the receiver and fell back against the wall. It was as if I had been physically shoved. I momentarily lost my balance and fell to the ground.

I gasped what I thought would be my last breath. Adrenaline then coursed through my body and I sprang to my feet. I fled out of the house and into the backyard. I was out of breath and shaking uncontrollably. I now knew without a doubt that I was in danger.

Sharon followed me into the backyard. "What on earth is going on?" she asked.

"Sharon, I got an electrical shock from the phone. We need to get out of here." I continued to shake.

No sooner were the words out of my mouth when the phone rang again. I wondered—again—how it could ring while it was off the hook. The ringing was so loud that it echoed throughout the house and into the backyard.

The expansive backyard and beautiful field belied the fact that demonic forces inhabited this place. I stood gazing back at the house and then stared at the balcony where it had all started that first night. I now understood the fight I heard that fateful night was over the destiny of my soul. *How could something so beautiful be so full of hate?* That's how I felt, hated by this home and its supernatural inhabitants. There was a force in this place that was literally from out of this world.

Sharon came to my side and said, "We'd better leave. It feels as if the house is going to blow up." The rumbling within the house could be heard outside. I was thankful Mrs. Jones and her brood had left.

With no sense of direction or purpose, we climbed into her car, and Sharon drove to where she was most comfortable—her church.

It was a country church, surrounded by cows, horses, and cornfields. There was a peace and serenity I instantly loved about the place. As soon as we walked in, I breathed in the smell of well-worn wood and a hint of mustiness found in buildings over a hundred years old. The floors creaked as we walked into the sanctuary. The church was cool and comfortable. Immediately, I felt peace wash over me, cleansing me of all anxiety and fear.

The stained-glass motifs of Jesus, Mary, and the crucifixion were so beautiful that tears filled my eyes. The beauty I beheld defied all description. I was touched and captivated by the way the sun lit up the angelic face of Jesus. When I gazed at the crucifixion panel, I started to weep. I had never felt such a connection to Jesus, and as I stared at His face, it was as if I felt His pain. I felt love emanate from the face I had seen all my life but never personally knew.

Sharon walked to the front of the church, and I followed her reluctantly. To me, this was sacred ground. I felt myself kneel on the steps and lay my head on the floor. For the first time in my life, I wanted to pray. I wanted to talk to God and hear what He had to say. Instinctively, I knew He had all the answers for me.

Ironically, prior to asking Jesus into my life, I thought I knew all the answers. I was the captain of my ship, and I would direct the course of my own destiny. Now I was weak, like a newborn. I could not walk unless held. I needed aid, and God would now lead me. I recognized that I was in a dangerous place, one that could destroy me. I was at the mercy of God and knew I needed the Savior.

I held my head in my hands and allowed the hard lump that had formed in my throat to materialize into a muffled cry. Suddenly, I felt remarkably comfortable there. I could not remember a time in my life when I felt that I belonged and was accepted as in this moment. Despite all my flaws and insecurities, I felt secure and loved here. Peace flooded all my being, and my mind became clear and receptive. Like a blind man seeing for the first time, I saw with greater clarity and precision a new dimension to life.

Then I heard Sharon's voice breaking the silence. "Lord, please protect us from these demonic forces. Jill needs to know that You are real and will protect her." Her voice sounded as if she were looking for relief from her burden—me.

The door opened to the sanctuary, and Sharon's prayer was interrupted by two older women I later learned worked in the church office. Their faces exuded faith, peace, and love.

"Oh, Sharon, sorry to interrupt you. We did not know who had come in," one of the ladies said.

"No, you're not interrupting," Sharon said. "Please come in. This is my friend, Jill. She's the one staying in the home that I talked to Pastor Don about last night. We really need to pray, and we'd like you to join us if you aren't too busy."

Unknown to me, Sharon had made a special trip to the church last night to find answers for me and her. She came to one who would know—her pastor.

They sat down, and we made an informal semi-circle. I briefly told them what had been happening at the house. Although it had only been a week since I started house-sitting, it felt like I had a lived a lifetime of experiences there. They gently inquired about the situation as if they were trying not to offend or hurt me. Just like with Pastor Don, I told them about all the weird happenings, and they sat listening intently. The women seemed to sense that I was looking for some type of an explanation.

"I think you're pretty special," said the thinner one whose glasses teetered on the end of her nose. "God is allowing you to see faith in action."

I did not feel special, but rather harassed and angry. *If God loves me and will protect me, why isn't He doing it now?* On the one hand, I knew Jesus was there to protect me, but on the other I was angry with God for letting this happen so protection would even be necessary. I was clearly a mess.

One of them asked me a simple question: "Do you pray for protection?"

To me, praying was a form of petitioning God when I had tried everything else in my life, but without success. It was not something I was accustomed to doing except in times of duress. Prayer was a last resort usually accompanied by a feeling of defeat, so it served no purpose in my life.

I cleared my throat. "How do I pray for protection when I don't even know how to pray, period? Can you tell me what you mean?"

A slightly plump lady held out her lovely white hands. "We will pray *for* you."

All of them grabbed hands—gnarled ones, chapped ones, well-manicured ones, along with my farm-worn ones. Their prayers began.

"Lord, we know You love us . . . and that includes Your daughter Jill . . . ."

"Please guard her from the demons that seem to be attacking her . . . ."

"Build a hedge of thorns around her, would You, Jesus?"

It sounded so simple, like they were having a conversation with a friend.

Although we had been at the church for hours, it felt like only fifteen minutes when the thin lady said, "Amen."

Then they made me memorize the verse that offered the best protection: "He who is in me is greater than he who is in the world" (1 John 4:4). "Say it at all times," said a tall woman with hair like steel. "But especially when you're afraid."

"Jesus will be your greatest weapon against all demonic powers," the lady with the lovely hands added.

The other woman squeezed *my* hand. "Remember, Jill, there is no greater power on earth, in heaven, or in hell than Jesus Christ! He can conquer anything, and through Him you can overcome and conquer!"

I didn't want this soothing sensation to leave. When Sharon reminded me that she had to get back home, I experienced the old feelings of trepidation. The church represented peace—a feeling that had eluded me all week—and it was wonderful! I felt encapsulated in a warm embrace by someone who loved me. For the first time in my life I felt loved, protected, and safe.

It was late in the afternoon when we left that little church and its safe haven. I had to feed the horses. Sharon drove back slowly. The winding roads and cow-pocked fields emanated peace, but it seemed the closer we got to Beth's house, the rawer and exposed I felt. Anxiety crept back, and my neck stiffened. Fearful thoughts began to race through my mind, and I wondered what would happen when we got there.

We drove up to the barn. The winding driveway only added to my terror with each turn. I knew I had to feed the horses and put them back into their stalls. As we walked into the barn, the coolness of the setting sun allowed a hush to settle on the horses, and the sound of them eating their grain and hay was music to my ears. Nothing happened. No phone ringing, no bees stinging me—nothing but an eerie stillness. Maybe it really was over.

I thanked Sharon for all her help and got into my car. The drive back to Delaware with the dogs seemed to take minutes. As I unlocked my door, I saw the glistening hardwood floors along with the perfect and perky pillows piled on the couch, just beckoning me to grab a book and read.

Instead, I grabbed my journal and wrote down all that I had experienced. I jotted the verse that the church ladies told me to memorize, "He who is in me is greater than he who is in the world." I kept repeating the verse, and slowly I began to believe the words were true.

Spent, exhausted, and weary, I quickly washed up. But before going to bed, I wanted to read the Bible. The only one I had was *The Good News Bible*, a contemporary version written for teens in easy-to-understand language, given initially to my brother when he joined our church. He had given it to me. Now it was my most beloved possession, not just because my brother gave it to me, but because of what had just happened in that circle of ladies.

I climbed into bed with it and pulled the covers tight to my body. There was a chill in the air. I kept reading Psalms, the biblical poems that gave me comfort and peace. I marveled at the wisdom I found in these short verses. Each verse helped me to feel peace and protection, and I started to believe what I had scoffed at just a few days earlier.

Before I knew it, my eyes began to droop, so I laid the Bible down next to my pillow on the bed. I fell soundly asleep and stayed asleep the whole night. It was the first straight eight hours of sleep I had gotten in a week.

As I slept, I had dreams that were full of peace, love, and protection. For the first time in my life, I did not feel that overwhelming sense of loneliness. Instead, I was full and content with the love I knew that could only have come from having Jesus in my life. Although I had searched for this feeling before through accomplishments, relationships with men, and a full, productive life, it had proved elusive.

How easily, though, I had found it in a book I thought was antiquated and outdated. I loved what I thought I would hate—church, the Bible, and Jesus Christ. This life as a Christian seemed to be something I had always wanted but chose to run away from. Now my life had a purpose and meaning, and as Pastor Don told me, I was being born again.

Chapter 3

~~~

As I awoke, peace and harmony flooded the room and bathed my being. Sleepily, I rolled over and rubbed my eyes. The sun was dancing cheerfully and showered the room with a dazzling sheen. Tiny sparrows flitted amongst the magnolia trees outside my window and chirped for an audience of one—me. It seemed as if my senses were on high alert, so everything was more intense and profound. I focused on this new heightened sense of reality available to all who accept Christ as their Savior. It seems there are many benefits to becoming a born-again Christian.

Admittedly, I am an anxious person by nature, so I relished this newfound peace. Not wanting this feeling to leave, I decided to lounge in bed and read the Bible, which I had placed next to me before I went to sleep. Lazily, I flung my arm next to me and felt around for the paperback Bible. However, patting the bed, looking under the covers, and lifting the pillow were to no avail. The Bible wasn't there. *Weird*, I thought. I knew I had put it next to me before I went to sleep. Where could it have gone?

Suddenly, my newfound peace was shattered. Frustrated, I got up, violently throwing my legs over the side of the bed. This scared Amy, and she quickly came to my side, sensing that something was wrong. Sheepishly, she wagged her tail and followed me into the living room. I was going to retrace my steps from the previous night. I knew that the Bible had been in my room before I went to bed. It could not move on its own. I scratched my head, pondering its disappearance.

I checked each room. After searching exhaustively in all possible places, the Bible could be, I flopped on the bed. Then, like a lightning bolt, an idea struck me: maybe it was on the floor.

I got on my knees and bent low to look under the bed skirt. *Could it be there?* I lay on my stomach and craned my neck to find the missing Bible. To my great relief, it lay upside down with the pages creased. It was under the middle of the bed, and I could not reach it. I sprawled on my belly to recover it. Once I reached it, I carefully flattened out the rumpled pages. Like a frightened child, I held the Bible up to my chest and rocked back and forth.

How had the Bible gotten under the bed? Why was it upside down and so rumpled? I reasoned, if it had fallen, it would be next to the bed. *What made it go under the bed?* I was baffled. *Did some demonic force move it while I innocently slept?*

Gingerly, I turned again to the Psalms. It seemed as if the Bible would naturally turn to these wonderful and powerful verses that filled me with awe. I was struck by the protection that was given to David, the writer of the Psalms. These verses mimicked my life. Frequently, David was fearful, fretful, and anxious. But when his focus shifted to God Almighty, it seemed that his fear, anxiety, and anger dissipated like a vapor.

I was struck by the fact that God can do anything. Slaying enemies, providing food and shelter, comforting the anxious, and allaying fears were always simple matters for the all-powerful, all-knowing God to accomplish. God could do anything if I believed and put my focus on Him.

It was my second to last day to go to the farm and take care of the horses. The usual forty-minute drive seemed only to take ten. I was lost in thought, reflecting on everything that happened in the past week, while the dogs panted in the seat next to me.

Verses from the Bible had infiltrated my mind, and I meditated on them. I was observing everything that happened to me from an outsider's point of view—not like it had really happened to me.

I marveled that I was not listening to music. Enjoying the classic rock station always got me to my destination. Instead, I discovered that the silence was not only necessary but refreshing as well. The silence enabled me to absorb, reflect, and learn. Like a song stuck in my head, verses from the Bible or words from Pastor Don echoed in my mind. I was making sense out of what could never have made sense before.

One aspect of what was going on was becoming glaringly apparent to me—I did not feel alone anymore. Ever since I prayed the salvation prayer with Pastor Don, there was something different about me. In the past, I had heard people speak about Jesus as a friend. This concept was inconceivable for me to understand. How could Jesus be a friend when you cannot see or hear Him? Yet the awareness of a comforting presence of an instant friend in my life began the day I asked Jesus into my heart.

As I entered the gravel driveway to the farm, I could feel paralyzing fear wash over me, and I knew I needed to pray. I prayed what I thought was the most juvenile prayer ever uttered: "God, I need You to help me. I hope the house does not blow up or catch on fire. Please protect Sharon and me. Thank You. Amen."

I did not know how to pray eloquently. I recalled the women from the church and how they prayed. They kept their prayers simple, and yet they were weighty and insightful. I hoped this prayer of mine would work. I glanced over at my Bible in the passenger's seat and patted it for reassurance. It was something tangible to go along with my feelings. I desperately wanted to read it for some much-needed advice.

As I put the car in park, I glanced at an upper window of the house and saw the curtain move as if someone were peering out. Oh, how I hated this place. Then I noticed Sharon's car parked in the distance. It seemed as if she wanted to park as far from the house as possible.

I got out of my car and stretched my legs. Glancing at the window as if it were my enemy, I screamed, "He who is in me is greater than he who is in the world!" I wanted every demonic power to know that they weren't going to mess with me anymore because He who is in me is none other than Jesus Christ.

I smirked over my newfound confidence. I thought, *This is another perk of having Jesus live in my heart* as I clicked off a mental list in my head of all the benefits of having Jesus as my personal Savior.

Sharon was still in her car, and I saw her head bob up when she heard me yell. With her head bowed, I knew she was either reading her Bible or praying. She looked up at me as she saw me walking toward her car. Her face showed exhaustion and fear. I knew if I believed Jesus was with me, He would be. I knew He would not let us down since He was there protecting us. I was buoyed by this newfound faith, and I felt I could throw her a life jacket of hope too.

Sharon slowly put her Bible down in her lap. She did not move, except to stare up at me with her crystal blue eyes that were now red and weary. The car window was down, and her hair rustled in the cool morning breeze.

"Sharon, you're not going to believe this! I didn't think I had a Bible, but I did! It was in my bookcase. I read it all night. Some pretty awesome things in there!"

Sharon slowly opened the door of her car as if it weighed a million pounds. Weakly, she pulled her legs out and grasped onto the door frame to lift her body.

"Sharon, what's wrong?" I asked, staring at her. She looked frail. Her hair was disheveled, and mascara streaked under her left eye.

The tightness in her face softened slightly. It was apparent that something was wrong, and even though her lips parted, nothing came out of her mouth. I grabbed her by the shoulders and asked her again what was wrong. Looking deeply into her eyes, I was searching for an answer.

"What happened?" I asked.

"*It* attacked me last night. When I left the farm last night, the engine light came on. I took my car right to the mechanic, and he said that nothing was wrong. He fixed the light, but no sooner had I driven out of the parking lot than the light came on again. I couldn't sleep, there were strange noises in my house, and I felt weird things too." She closed her eyes as if she were trying to shut out what had happened.

"It" was an unnamed force that seemed bent on evil, torture, confusion, and fear. We had both felt its presence. It was not like anything we had ever experienced before. I was sorry for ever involving Sharon in this weird and terrifying situation.

"Sharon," I said, "go home. You don't need to help me. Go home. I will be all right by myself." I was lying. I didn't think I would be, but I had to make an offer. My heart broke because I knew that what was attacking me was now attacking her. It was my fault, and I felt bad about it.

The old me was reappearing—cocky, self-assured, and feeling in control. No longer was I feeling helpless. Instead, I was feeling powerful and capable. This was a power I had never experienced before because a feeling of comfort and peace was attached to it. I knew if I could say that verse about Christ being in me, it would give me the strength to combat these forces.

"No, I'll stay. I'm already here anyway," Sharon said as we walked to the barn. She wore open-toed sandals and blue linen shorts with a white seersucker shirt. It brought out the blue in her eyes, and she looked as if she was ready for a morning sail on a yacht—not a battle with demonic forces.

I was instantly relieved that she agreed to stay. I liked having Sharon there. I was becoming confused easily with the lack of sleep and everything that was going on, so I was messing up on the feeding instructions and medications for the horses. Sharon's clarity of mind was just what I needed.

Feeding twenty horses approximately ten different feeds and numerous supplements and medications is not for the timid or inexperienced. Horses, despite their large and muscular frames, are extremely fragile. Too much, too little, or incorrect feed can make them seriously ill. These were pampered show horses that some people hocked their homes to purchase. There also were bold warmbloods imported from Germany and Switzerland. I knew too well my responsibilities. Sharon was my checker, and she was very thorough. Her nursing background was perfect for the job that was at hand.

The horses heard our voices and started to whinny, paw, and pace in anticipation of their feed. This was music to a horse lover's ears. Their cute and inquisitive faces were irresistible as they peered over their stall doors. We went into the feed room and turned on the lights. This was the first time the lights did not flicker, and I marveled at the fact that I could actually see what I was doing. There weren't any noises, distractions, bees, or phones ringing. It was quiet and there was peace. I felt protected. The sound of horses eating their hay and feed with no other sounds interfering was the sweetest sound in the world to me.

Then we both stopped mid-aisle. We both heard it, the faint sound of humming. "It" had come out to the barn. That sound had only been heard in the house. We looked at each other. I was sad to admit it, but I felt defeated. I thought that as soon as I accepted Jesus as my Savior and I was born again, this nonsense would stop. I wanted to cry in frustration. Where was God now?

I said in the fiercest voice I had, "He who is in me is greater than he who is in the world! Get out of here! You have no right! Jesus is here, and you cannot be here! Now, get out!"

Silence! It worked. Sharon and I did a high five and danced around each other in a mock victory dance. This was marvelous. We felt peace restored and most important, we both felt protected. My declaration revealed that we did have power—not from us, but from Jesus Christ. If I spoke the name of Jesus Christ, the demonic forces had to leave.

Sharon and I continued to feed the horses, dole out their individual medicines, and give them their shots. We were operating with such smooth precision that we finished in record time. We let the horses out into their paddocks. The sun was bright, and it felt good to be here with them. I was suddenly very grateful to be a part of this farm. It allowed me to imagine what it would be like if I had a farm of my own, a dream that I had since I was a child. Staying here for a week and taking care of the horses enabled me to live it out.

I marveled at this multi-million-dollar estate. The twenty-stall barn came furnished with a tack-and-feed room large enough to be a small house, a bathroom, a state-of-the-art wash stall for the horses complete with a vacuum, and an office. There was an indoor riding ring large enough to hold a circus, along with a dressage ring, cross-country course, outdoor stadium jumping ring, and beautiful trails. It was a horse lover's paradise. The horses were given the best care, with automatic waterers that would cool the water in the summer and warm the water in the winter. No expense was spared. The stalls were cushioned with thick rubber mats, and the aisle had rubber on it to prevent the horses from slipping.

After we finished feeding the horses, we walked up to the house. It was built in the early 1800s by a wealthy business owner but had fallen into disrepair and neglect when the original owners died. It was during this period of abandonment when rumors surfaced that the home was haunted because it had been broken into and Satan worshippers would conduct séances and hold meetings there.

It was undeniable that all who saw the house would leave with an uneasy feeling. The shutters hung in precarious positions that would bang with the slightest breeze. The porch hung off the side of the house. The windows were broken, and the open back door would knock and thud. This house would make anyone who visited shiver because an uneasy and unsettled feeling hung over it that couldn't be denied.

Beth was beautiful in a simple and natural way. Her golden blonde hair hung down to her shoulders in soft waves that framed her heart-shaped face. Her green-blue eyes were so unusual that it was often the first thing anyone would notice about her. She seemed to have the perfect life. Her husband appeared doting and kind. Although he was always working, as soon as he came into the house, he would grab her and kiss her in a fun and playful way. You could tell that they complemented each other, and in my mind, they made the perfect couple.

I started to ride her beautiful large horse, Schimmer. He was jet black with a small white star on his intelligent, broad face. He was a Trakehner, a breed rumored to come from a royal bloodline. By the way Schimmer acted, I knew it was the truth. He enjoyed long, luxurious grooming before he was worked or ridden. You could not haphazardly brush him and throw on the tack because he would turn and glare at you until he was properly brushed and fussed over. He was so self-important that he insisted on being first to be fed as well as first to be let out in the field of his choosing, and you had to feed him warm bran mashes on Sundays. He expected impeccable manners from his riders. You also had to be firm but respectful. If you showed any weakness, he capitalized on it. Schimmer was also flighty and fractious, enjoying the surprise of upsetting his rider, especially me.

Since I was only five feet tall and a hundred pounds, this horse realized that he had many advantages over me, and he reminded me daily of his superiority. An example of his royal attitude was the way he would dump me and then stand next to me with a sheepish face as if he were saying, "Geez, I do not know how that happened." Secretly, he was chuckling and so were all his friends, two goats and a small pony that would gather at the ring fence and watch the hilarious show he put on every time I rode him.

Many days I coaxed him into his smooth and joyous canter. We floated through the air, and his long legs thundered rhythmically over the earth. He snorted with every stride. I allowed my hips to roll in perfect synchronicity with his powerful strides, movements which lulled me into believing that he would not dump me. Ever so slightly he dropped his shoulder as we rounded a corner, and before I could react, the inevitable happened: my short legs were not able to hold on, and I landed in a heap slightly on the inside of the ring. He stopped instantaneously, hovering over me and nuzzling my very red face. He glanced over at his friends, and I could almost hear them laughing over my wild acrobatic leaps and flops. Then he pressed his head onto my shoulder as if willing me to get up and give it a go again.

Beth thought it was funny too, but her children found it hysterical. They sat on the fence and hollered to me that I needed to go faster. They knew once I got Schimmer to canter, he would do what he did best— humiliate me. They giggled and laughed and sometimes yelled, "Do it again, Jill!"

"What? Are you guys crazy? Once a day is enough for me!" I said, jumping back on Schimmer and finishing with a gallop across the field. They loved seeing us flying across the field, where he was always the perfect gentleman, leaving me with the sense that this guy was way too smart to just be a horse. Everyone believed that he was the king, and I believed it too.

After I rode her horse, Beth often invited me in for tea, much to the delight of her children. They loved the added attention that I gave them, and she enjoyed the adult companionship. We began a comfortable relationship and gradually revealed our dreams and hopes, as well as our troubles, to one another.

It was during one of these times that I shared with Beth my vision of someday teaching handicapped children how to ride, using the horses as therapy. As a special education teacher by day, I volunteered and worked on my certification at night to be an equine therapist. After my first visit to the certification program, I knew that I was meant to be an equine therapist.

As I divulged my dream of owning a farm to someday conduct equine therapy, Beth's eyes lit up and she grabbed my hand. "This is exactly what I want to do too!" she told me.

Beth asked if I would be willing to teach at her new farm until I got a facility of my own. I assured her that would be my greatest pleasure. Her newly acquired mansion and property allowed her to realize her dream. It also confirmed mine of teaching these special-needs children, so they could experience the unbridled freedom that comes with riding.

For two years, Beth and her husband spent countless hours putting time and money into this long-neglected and abandoned home. Eventually it was restored to its original majesty and updated with the best there was in appliances and modern conveniences. Her kitchen had beautiful granite countertops, gorgeous cabinetry, and wide-width plank floors. No expense was spared. She collected antiques to complement the time period of the home, and she even refurbished a twelve-foot antique crystal chandelier that she hung in the dining room. The antiques were put in the front parlors, and she accented the rooms with Oriental rugs, sterling silver candelabras, and stained-glass windows.

This home became the talk of the town as it was slowly renovated and converted from a rundown property characterized by abject neglect into a showplace of grandeur. Then Beth began outfitting the outside of the property with the state-of-the-art barn and arenas. She hired only the best architects, engineers, builders, and journeymen, who began the laborious tasks of moving earth for creating proper drainage and developing perfect sites for riding rings and barns.

Next, she quickly hired me to teach riding lessons. I was only too eager to begin my dream job of teaching riding lessons to her first few students. It was a dream for me that was coming true, thanks to my friendship with Beth.

It was our friendship that led her to ask me to house-sit at her home and farm while she and her family took a much-needed vacation. Yet little did she or I know that what she asked me to do would be impossible.

———*∾*———

Chapter 4

After that first day of being born again, I no longer needed an alarm to wake up. Despite my belief that Jesus was in me, I slept fitfully, tossing and turning throughout the night. At times I felt a strange uneasy presence, an eerie spirit in *my* home—not just Beth's. When truly frightened, I would silently utter the name of Jesus, and then a warm blanket of peace would cover me and permeate the atmosphere. I wished I didn't have to do this over and over, that the peace would just stay.

Sharon was still meeting me at the farm at six o'clock in the morning to feed the horses and put them out. On the third day, I quickly threw on clothes, washed my face, brushed my teeth, and—as if it were an afterthought—prayed. I picked up the Bible that was on the bedside table. "Thank God it hasn't moved," I muttered to myself.

I began to feel uneasy. *If nothing happened last night, what were the demons saving up for today?*

Hastily, I threw on britches, boots, and a T-shirt and pulled my hair back into a ponytail. Holding the Bible to my chest and wrestling with an apple half in my mouth and half out while trying to call Amy to jump into the back seat of the car, I laughed at myself for always trying to do too much. Amy yelped at the thought of going on an adventure. Boots and britches to her meant long trail rides, and she loved roaming in the woods while I rode my horse. She wagged her tail in anticipation and licked my hand.

My little car roared to life, and I placed the Bible on the seat next to me. I grabbed the apple with one hand while driving with the other. Slowly I drove out of my neighborhood and, after making one quick stop, onto the highway that would carry me to the gorgeous countryside of New Jersey. The miles drew me closer to the place I had come to hate. With each passing mile, my heart began to race, and peace was replaced with anxiety. My hands began to sweat, and little beads of perspiration also appeared on my forehead. It was becoming apparent that this farm was not only affecting me spiritually but physically as well.

As I drove past the home and onto the barn driveway, I felt fear in the pit of my stomach. Nauseous, I gagged to keep from throwing up. Sharon's car was already there, as usual. She had her head bowed, and I realized that just like every day, she was reading her Bible.

I half-smiled, and she smiled back as if she were a mirror. We were going where we did not want to go, and I sighed as she swung open her car door. She got out looking like a cool breeze in a crisp white sleeveless shirt and royal blue shorts with a ruby red belt. Her face was flushed, and I knew that she was still feeling as much anxiety as me.

The horses heard our footsteps approaching the barn door, and they began to whinny. The big, bold Thoroughbreds pawed at their stall mats, insisting on being fed first. The quarter horses waited patiently, but the ponies were trying to open their stall doors. I laughed at how the breeds of the horses revealed their personalities, not only in their care, but also in how they worked while being ridden. I answered their neighs with a resounding, "Good morning, guys and gals!"

They nickered their acknowledgement, and I started laying out the feed, supplements, hay, and medications. I efficiently began to roll the cart down the aisle to feed my persistent four-legged charges. Some shook their head, frustrated that I was not moving as quickly as they liked. I was getting a serious horse tongue-lashing, and I laughed at their antics.

When we were finished feeding the horses, Sharon produced another gorgeous breakfast of piping hot biscuits with homemade strawberry jam that her mother had made. I pulled up two stools and we used a feed barrel as our table. I found a red-and-white checkered dish towel that had been freshly washed and put it on our makeshift table. Sharon laughed at my silly table, and I told her that this was a high-class place. To her surprise, I produced a steaming hot latte for her that I had bought at the coffee café in the quaint little town just south of Beth's home. Gingerly, she sipped the latte, and I began to spread a huge mound of the rich strawberry jam on a biscuit. I was being greedy, and Sharon sarcastically said that I should weigh a million pounds with all the food I ate. We sat munching happily on our breakfast when suddenly we heard footsteps in the barn.

I got up and opened the feed room door to find one of my students there for an early morning ride. Anna was a beautiful college student whose parents had surprised her with an early graduation gift of a package of riding lessons. Frequently, she would show up an hour early to help with the horses, and I enjoyed her eagerness and helpfulness.

We offered her a biscuit, so she hopped over the counter and grabbed one. Anna talked incessantly about her love of horses and then asked if she could help us turn the horses out after they ate. Sharon smiled with the relief of knowing she would not have to do a thing on this beautiful morning.

"Of course, I would love the help!" I said as I started to grab some lead ropes.

"Great! Who should I take first?" Anna practically vaulted into the aisle next to the feed room. I felt a momentary misgiving. *What if something strange happened?* But her enthusiasm was so contagious, I put it out of my mind.

"Hmmm . . . how about you take this end and I take that one?" I pointed to the lesson horses for her and the boarder horses for me.

"Sure!" she shouted as she opened the stall doors and gingerly took out the lesson horses.

I smiled, remembering the time when everything with a horse was a great experience for me. The newness of being with these majestic animals brought meaning and purpose to my life.

Katie, the newest instructor, walked in as we finished putting the last horse out. I still had to make the trek to the house to take care of the little critters.

"Katie, take over for me for a minute, would you?" I asked.

She answered with a beaming smile.

Sharon and I made our way up to the house while Amy and Alfred went running and spinning in the morning dew. As I turned the key in the door, I could hear deafening music. Sharon and I glanced at each other with foreboding. The music was a combination of rap, heavy metal, and classical music playing simultaneously.

Once inside the door, I ran across the beautiful cherry hardwood floors to the stereo encased in an ornate oak cabinet. I opened the door and turned the receiver off. Silence was restored, and we both sighed in relief until I said, "How did that turn on when no one was here?

"I fed the hamsters and the squeaky guinea pig and petted them, for they seemed extremely upset. I wondered out loud how long they had been subject to this racket. Then I swept the floor and vacuumed while Sharon played with the dogs. Amy and Alfred enjoyed each other as they hurtled and sprinted after the ball that Sharon tirelessly tossed to them.

Glancing at the clock, I realized it was time for me to teach my first lesson. I locked the door and set the alarm once again in the house. Teaching is a gift, and one that I cultivated through the trials and tribulations of being a special education teacher. Patience, trust, empathy, and communication are the characteristics of an excellent teacher, and I wanted nothing more than to foster them in my classroom and the riding ring. My students not only learned to ride, but they also learned the art of communicating with a horse by paying attention to the nuances of the horse's lips, ears, and body language. I grew in my knowledge too, for many of my adult students would ask poignant questions that would lead me to see things in a new way. I respected them, and they respected me. It was a position I held in the highest regard. And at that point, at least I could feel confident about that.

Sharon decided to leave, and I hugged her hard.

"Sharon," I said, "thank you for all that you have done for me!"

"No worries! Hey, I'll call you later, okay?"

"Sure!"

She got into her car, and I watched her as she drove down the long gravel driveway. I wished I'd had her faith as long as she had. Maybe this wouldn't even be happening if I had.

Then I began my full lesson schedule. Hours turned into minutes. At the end of the day, as the last lesson student was leaving, I heard the unmistakable sound of Sharon's SUV pulling up to the barn. I glanced out the big barn doors to see her pull out a wicker basket.

"Hey, Jill!" she called out.

"Sharon, what are you doing here?"

"I thought you could use a little food," she said, opening the lid of the basket to show the chicken salad on thick Italian bread along with potato chips.

"Sharon, you shouldn't have!" I laughed.

"I was a little bored and thought you might enjoy a sandwich by now," she said, glancing at her watch. It was four in the afternoon.

"Hey, let's eat this feast at the house, like normal people!" I said, grabbing the basket from her arms.

"Sounds like a plan!" she said.

We began to walk up to the house.

"Do you hear that?" Sharon asked.

"What?"

We both stopped walking and listened intently.

"Is that music?"

"Yes!" I almost screamed.

We both knew what it was: the stereo was on again, with all three radio stations merging into a cacophony of sound that would wake the dead.

I ran to the house, opened the door, deactivated the alarm, and slid across the room to turn off the receiver.

Silence. After Sharon came in, we both chuckled uneasily. I didn't want her to see that I was still afraid.

"Was someone in here while we were gone?" Sharon asked.

"No, it would be impossible because I set the alarm," I said.

Sharon and I stood at the kitchen island, unsure of what we should do, when we heard someone knocking at the back door. Sharon had lost all color in her face, and I felt sick to my stomach. I wondered who could be knocking at the door.

After deliberating long enough to force the person to knock again, this time louder, I opened the door. It was Laura, a friend of Beth's. I was relieved that she wasn't a demon who came to call, but I was immediately uneasy. If she found out what was going on here, she'd tell Beth, and I didn't want that. I put on a plastic smile.

"Hi! Come in!" I said.

"I just wanted to see how you were making out," she said as she brushed past me.

"Great!" I said, too cheerily. "Sharon's here. Come on in. We'll have a party."

Even though they were ten years apart, Beth considered Laura her best friend. Laura was the polar opposite of Beth. Whereas Beth was petite with aristocratic features, Laura was built like a bull: strong, bold, and loud with fiery dark eyes and long, unkempt, curly mahogany hair. Beth would think it, and Laura would say it. Laura held none of her thoughts back, and her remarks were as colorful as her clothing. Many times, I was bent over in hysterics after listening to Laura's unabashed interpretations of everyday annoyances and observations.

Laura usually stayed at Beth's house when they went on vacation, and the only reason I had been asked to stay this time was that Laura was unavailable. Laura pulled up a chair and peered inside the basket.

"Mmmm, looks good!" she said.

"We were just about to eat. Would you like some?" I asked.

"I sure would!"

I split my sandwich and grabbed paper plates while Sharon poured iced tea and put out napkins. Laura began to greedily bite into the sandwich. She wiped her mouth and dipped her hand into the chips.

Sharon and I sneaked a secretive glance at one another in amazement. We had never seen anyone eat so quickly in our lives. As I watched her chow down, I came to a decision. If there was anyone who knew about this house, it would be Laura, and she would not be afraid to share with us what she knew. I tentatively broached the subject.

"Hey, Laura, when you stayed here, did you ever feel anything strange? Did you ever experience anything abnormal? Like, did the stereo ever go on without being touched? Or would lights go on seemingly by themselves?"

She stopped munching and looked me in the eye.

"What do you mean?" she asked.

I knew whatever I said to Laura would go right back to Beth. I started to retrace my steps.

"Like, is the stereo on a timer? Are the lights on timers? I mean, sometimes the stereo and lights turn on at certain times, and I was wondering if they were on timers."

I was not usually quick on my feet but was proud of myself for coming up with the "timer" excuse.

"No, nothing is on timers," she replied. "Though I don't really know. But nothing went on when I was here."

"Oh," I said, "I was just wondering."

"Man, I loved staying here! Did you get a chance to use the hot tub?" she asked.

"No, not yet," I said.

"Man, you have to! The jets are amazing! Hey, I gotta run!" She was already throwing her plate away as she headed for the door. "Thanks for the sandwich! Take care."

With a slam of the door, she was gone.

Maybe this was all just my imagination. Just maybe, I reasoned, the stereo was on a timer, the chairs did not move, the lights did not go on and off by themselves, and the house did not make any strange noises.

This house-sitting job had turned me into a woman who was on the brink of brokenness. But it was here that I learned to pray.

—~~—

Chapter 5

‑‑∿‑‑

S ue was a pillar of faith. She was an English teacher at the same high school where Sharon and I worked, and I had become friends with her through our mutual love of horses. She was always calm and reassuring. Her character portrayed a strong faith in God, and she had a deep, resounding assurance that God Himself was right beside her at all times.

Sharon and I knew that we needed another witness to the mysterious activities, as well as a spiritual force to help us with the now palpable hostility at this home. Sue was not only a mutual friend, but her faith and reassurance was also needed now.

After hearing the story of this home on the phone, Sue said, "You need Jesus Christ to save you from the demonic forces that inhabit the place. I'll come over and check it out." I heard her chuckle. "And I wouldn't mind giving you a hand with the animals."

Sharon and Sue planned to meet me in the driveway. Beth and her family would be arriving home later that evening, and I was anxious to get this business finished before they returned. Both Sharon and I were exhausted, so we needed another strong arm and bastion of faith to encourage us. Nothing ever seemed to bother Sue because she was always so steady in her approach to life. Whereas Sharon and I were anxious, Sue was the opposite—calm and relaxed. Full of wonder, Sue was excited to see this magnificent home and the horse facility.

Although it was early September, there was an uneasy chilliness in the air that afternoon. The wind swayed the two-hundred-year-old oak tree in front of the house, and its limbs rustled and creaked as if signaling a sense of doom. The manicured lawn, shrubs, and flowers enhanced the beauty of the home, but they seemed dull and lifeless for some reason that day. There was an obvious atmosphere of sadness that blanketed the property.

I got out of my car. My apprehension and fearfulness traveled down to my legs, and I paced back and forth along the driveway. Sharon was picking up Sue. If there was ever something that you could count on with Sue, it was that she was always late, and today was no exception. If the three of us were getting together, we would often tell white lies to Sue to get her there on time, and this included shaving an hour or two off the actual meeting time to ensure that Sue would be prompt.

As I heard the familiar roar of Sharon's powerful SUV climb the slope of the driveway, something caught my eye. The second-story window curtain of the house was swaying back and forth, even though there were no windows open. I felt a cold knot tightening in my stomach.

Sharon had a pained expression on her face as she parked her vehicle, yet Sue's green eyes crinkled in anticipation.

"Oh my, this is beautiful!" Sue exclaimed as she got out of the car and appraised the home and the expansive farm. She slowly spun around three hundred and sixty degrees, and with each sight she took in, she gasped.

Sue owned a farm with her husband, Jay, who raised steer, and she had a half a dozen horses herself. She giggled and swooned as if she was a young bride on her honeymoon every time she talked about her horses. She was one of those women who was obsessed with horses. The driving horses were for her husband, and the riding horses were hers.

They had a gorgeous property with a winding river and gazebo for her to escape the cares of life to write and journal. Her home had a comfortable ranch-style design with an expansive fireplace and hardwood floors. It was not unusual for atypical pets to call it home too. She had a baby swan that needed nursing, and she and Jay often watched TV at night with Larry, the swan. Then there were the other critters, like the baby squirrels and the tiny piglet runt. Sue always had a story about her life on the farm, and we spent many get-togethers listening to the colorful tales of Sue and the adventures on her farm.

Sue also had a mountain of faith. She was completely convinced that having the Lord in your life would get you through anything, and she had enough evidence from her own life to prove it.

Once, she decided to put out a huge thousand-pound round bale of hay for her hungry herd of bulls in their twenty-acre pasture. When feeding bulls, you cannot step foot out of your truck. The round bale of hay lay in the bed of the truck, so Sue put the truck window down and climbed onto the roof and down into the truck bed. Due to her movements in the truck bed, however, the truck began to lurch forward, and with a cry she realized that the truck's gear had somehow jumped out of park.

Off it rambled at twenty miles an hour down a hill. She clung to the side of the window, watching the herd of hungry bulls in hot pursuit. She did what she always does when she is in trouble—she prayed. With that, the truck veered sharply to the left and hit smack dab into the middle of a small sapling. God had answered her prayer by stopping the truck, just like she asked. She gingerly climbed back into the truck cab and drove back to the barn with another story of God's miraculous hand at work in her life.

Another time, she and her husband were doing their nightly routine of fence inspection. For a farmer, this is one of the most important jobs. A hole or damage to the fence meant precious livestock roaming loose, or worse, a bull causing a car accident. Every night, their routine after dinner involved inspecting the fence.

Jay drove the beat-up, rusty old Ford 250 because the passenger-side door had been bashed in by a mad bull and could no longer be opened. Sue, being spry and agile, just leaped into the window of the passenger's side like it was the normal way to get in to a truck. Jay periodically stopped if they saw anything amiss and directed Sue to fix certain pieces of the fence.

Sue never complained because she enjoyed being with Jay, and would laughingly refer to this time as their date. The twilight was a time of relaxation when they discussed their day. She talked about the woes of being a high school teacher, and he talked about his beloved bulls. They had a lot in common because they both loved their jobs and the children and animals that graced their lives.

On this particular night, Sue found a piece of the fence slightly damaged, and Jay stopped while she hopped out and began to bang in the uncooperative nails. Unbeknownst to them, however, one of the farm hands had not taken the bulls out of the pasture. Sue was so immersed in fixing the fence that she never heard Jay screaming until it was too late. The bull crashed into her bottom like a ton of fury, and she flew across the fence and landed on a soft mound of dirt on the other side. She lay in a heap, and her husband was convinced that she was dead. Just as he was ready to risk his own life and get out of the truck, she popped up and said, "I'm all right! It sure was the perfect spot to land!"

Sue giggled over God's wonderful provision in times of need. After bouncing up and down on the soft mound of earth and raising her hands to God in thanks, she brushed off her jeans and climbed back over the fence. Without touching the ground, she climbed into the passenger-side window, landing in the seat with the grace of a ballerina.

"Sue, you are amazing!" her husband, a man of few words, said.

She winked at him and then exclaimed, "No, God is!" She meant it too. It was God who protected her. To Sue, there were no chance happenings. Instead, it was always God's great providence.

At work, everyone gathered around Sue to hear of her near misses with death or defeat. She always ended these stories with, "God really saved me that time."

Despite my own lack of belief, I'd always thought that there had to be some truth to this statement. I'd seen what bulls could do. After all, I had been to the rodeo before and seen many strong, athletic men taken out in an ambulance.

Sue was five feet two and a half inches (she always added the half-inch part) and maybe a hundred pounds wet. She was spry and remarkably strong for such a petite woman. Sue would have been out earlier in the week, except she had been bitten by a stray cat while doctoring its hurt leg and was in the hospital receiving IV antibiotics. I thought that she would be bored confined to a bed, but she laughed and explained that she was filling herself with the Word, the Bible. If Sue was not with the horses, her husband, or a small injured critter, she was in her gazebo praying, writing in her journal, or reading her worn and torn Bible that she carried like a badge of courage.

That afternoon, when Sue clasped her hands together, Sharon and I knew that she would say something profound. Sue was a natural leader. Her words of wisdom inspired and encouraged rough and hardened high school seniors bent on giving her a hard time in the classroom. By the end of the year, they were holding back tears because they would miss her and then wonder aloud how they would get through life without her. She would smile and say, "Go on, God has a plan for you."

Like her hardened seniors, we listened.

"We need to pray!" Sue said firmly as she grasped our hands out in the driveway.

I protested even though I had invited her over. I just wanted to get into this house one last time, take care of the animals, and then resume my quiet and uneventful life back in Delaware. *All of this would somehow go away*, I tried to convince myself. I was still not comfortable with prayer, and my bulldog personality at times clashed with Sue's quiet strength.

Sue began praying anyway. She and Sharon bowed their heads, but I was too agitated and distracted, so I stared intently at the house. Then something significant struck me as I heard Sue pray. She asked for a "hedge of protection," and I wondered silently what that meant. *Why did we need protection? Could we get hurt physically?* Fear coursed through my body.

When the amens had been said, the three of us walked to the back door. As I unlocked the door, we could hear a faint electrical hum vibrating through the house. At first barely audible, the noise became a loud static sound. Then we heard banging from the balcony upstairs that culminated in a loud, resounding thump, as if something had fallen. The thumping became louder as we walked into the kitchen.

Then it happened: one of the kitchen chairs scraped across the wooden floor, and it sent Sharon and me scampering into the mud room.

Sue was undeterred, and we stared at her with amazement behind the mud room door frame. Admiring the beauty of the house, she began exploring. We could hear her go into the dining room. Sharon and I couldn't help but admire her bravery and confidence. If Sue had not been with us, we would have dashed out of there on winged feet.

"My gosh, I have never seen such a large chandelier!" Sue exclaimed. "What exquisite carpets! This is a beautiful home."

She circled the dining room, obviously admiring the fine crown molding and silk lounge chairs in the sitting room. She clearly saw this as an opportunity to enjoy fine interior decorating, and nothing would dissuade her from taking it all in. I reassured myself that she was truly a strong person because the word *fear* was clearly not a part of her vocabulary. Living with the Lord and seeing all that He had accomplished in her life had given her an extraordinary self-assuredness that I wanted for myself.

The humming and banging was bursting to deafening levels. I was afraid of what would happen if we didn't leave immediately. It was then that I knew our very lives were at the mercy of this menacing power.

"Sue, let's go!" I said, grabbing Sharon's arm. We laughed, but only from sheer nervousness.

I put Alfred back into the house, set the alarm, and practically ran out of the house with Sharon, leaving Sue to close the door behind us. Laughing, we hugged each other and danced in relief that we had made it out unscathed.

"Sue is truly spiritual and connected to the Lord," Sharon said.

I nodded. "She actually seemed to *like* being in the house, even with all that humming and thumping and bumping going on."

Hastily, I made a retreat to my car and opened the door so quickly that I almost knocked Sue down as she was walking behind me. I jumped into the car and put the key into the ignition, signaling that I was ready to leave. Sue stood next to my door. She wanted to stay with me. She was walking with the Lord, and if there was one thing she was certain of, it was that I needed spiritual help.

But all I could think about was that I was only one turn of the key away from driving over the country roads and into my little town in Delaware. This nightmare would be a lifeless relic that I would place on my shelf of extraordinary life experiences. Maybe I would bring it up at future dinner parties, or perhaps Bible studies if someone was "open" to hearing about it.

Sue had other plans, however. As she leaned against my car, Sharon at her side, she was still savoring the beauty of the house.

"Don't go yet," she urged me through the car window as she began to quote Scriptures from memory. Her face was lit up with enthusiasm as she recalled specific verses. She clasped her hands together in reverence as she spoke the verses. She would pause and put her finger up to her chin, trying to recall a particularly good verse to read when one was in trouble and needed reassurance. I thought perhaps she knew that I needed these verses, so maybe this journey was not over yet.

Meanwhile, my mind fantasized about taking a warm bath, sleeping in my luxurious bed, and getting ready for another busy school year. I was miles away mentally. Sue read my face, and she began to step back from the car. With my fingers on the ignition and foot on gas, I was ready to leave—when again something caught my attention.

I peered closely and noticed something shimmering was covering Sue's heart. It looked like prisms of light rotating and spinning.

Inside each prism was a tiny dark body that glowed. Upon closer inspection, I saw tiny warrior angels, for their faces were expressions of determination and strength. With fury, they hovered around Sue's heart. She moved her arms, and it seemed that these miniature angels multiplied. I stared with a gaping mouth. My eyes became lasers deciphering what was before me. It was supernatural, like this home and barn—it was not of this world.

My mind raced and then slowed, trying to make sense of what I was seeing. I glanced over at Sharon and noticed that these angels were fluttering around her heart too. Their translucent bodies were taut with readiness to protect her from danger. Sharon lifted her arm, and I saw the little angels swarm around her arms. I glanced back at Sue. I realized that they had made a hedge of protection around both women. I looked at my car and observed that they had formed a hedge of protection around my car as well. They fluttered around and across each woman.

What Sue had prayed for had become a reality. Incredulously, I looked to the sky to see a funnel of angels being majestically called by prayer coming down to us, the source being heaven itself. Sue gazed into my eyes through the car window, and she knew that I was seeing something. It was another confirmation that God had heard our prayer and sent exactly what we needed.

"Jill, what do you see?" she asked.

"Sue, you are not going to believe what I'm seeing!"

"An angel?"

A laugh, wild and free, burst from me. "A legion of angels has formed a protective hedge around your heart and upper body, and they have literally formed a hedge that extends to Sharon and onto my car!"

"I can feel them, I really can!" Sharon said. "It feels like tiny kisses on my arms!"

"Move your arms!" I called out.

They began moving their arms, jumping and shouting, spinning and twirling. Every movement was accompanied by a flurry of these tiny fighter angels. They were not exactly what I thought angels would look like, but there was no denying that they truly were a hedge of protection. I glanced toward heaven and saw them fill the sky.

"Your face, Jill! You should see your face!" Sue exclaimed.

"What's wrong with my face?" I craned my neck to see my face in the rearview mirror. My face was glowing as if a lamp had been lit on the inside.

For three glorious days after that, total strangers stopped me and told me that I was beautiful, because I was so filled with spiritual light. I had so much energy that I could only sleep for a few hours each night. With this newfound energy, I delved into the Bible to discover limitless lessons, and now glorious Christian music filled my home.

I knew this journey of discovery would be one of supernatural wonders and confirmations that God was with me. It marked the beginning of the ways the Lord would reveal Himself in the days and weeks to come.

Leaving behind dread and danger, I looked forward to peace and tranquility, though much of what I found was all that I hated, lurking to lure me into despair.

But I knew that God had other plans.

Chapter 6

⸺〰⸺

The winding roads and picturesque landscape popped with brilliant greens, reds, and yellows as I drove home that night. I passed by open fields, stone homes, and farms, trying to digest this experience. Mentally, I made a checklist of everything I had experienced and concluded it had to be divine intervention. It was God revealing Himself, and that shattered and reconstructed my sense of reality.

My house sat in the middle of an old, well-established development with beautiful magnolia trees which still held their blooms like little parachutes waiting to float to the ground. My home was like a welcoming lighthouse in a port of peace, so different now from what it had been last week.

I hastily hung up my jacket and took off my muddy boots in the laundry room. Pulling back my hair, I glanced in the mirror at my face in the bathroom. I saw what Sue and Sharon had seen—that same shimmering glow. Smiling sheepishly at my reflection, I felt as if I had just won the Olympic gold, but it was better than a gold medal. I had won the ultimate prize, for God was with me and I was immersed in His glorious power. His Word said that He would never leave me, and after seeing the angels, I knew that this was a confirmation.

Hurtling to my bed like my horse diving into his feed bin, I looked forward to settling down with the Bible and allowing all that I experienced to process through my overactive mind. I plumped the pillows and arranged them, so I could lean back and read in comfort the verses Sue had told me to read when I got home. Fumbling with the pages, I landed on verse after verse that seemed to speak specifically to me. I kept reading Psalm 3 repeatedly, each time gleaning a different teaching. My mind was draped with peace like a fresh soft blanket of snow.

> But you, Lord, are a shield around me,
> my glory, the One who lifts my head high.
> I call out to the Lord,
> and He answers me from His holy mountain.
>
> I lie down and sleep;
> I wake again, because the Lord sustains me.
> I will not fear though tens of thousands
> assail me on every side

Suddenly, the room exploded when the phone rang. Without picking it up, I knew who was calling. I quickly prayed for God's words to fill my mouth. It was Beth, and she would have questions about my stay. So, with gravity, I prepared to face her anger. Just a few hours earlier, I had penned a note to her, explaining in vague language what happened while she was gone.

Instead of, "Hi, Jill," she launched into, "What is this? . . . . You could not stay at my house because you felt uncomfortable?'

"Beth—" I tried to say.

But she wasn't having it. "What could possibly make you feel uncomfortable? My house is six thousand square feet of state-of-the-art beauty and opulence. How could you possibly feel uncomfortable staying here? I want to know!"

Beth's anger vibrated through my being, dismantling my fragile sense of peace.

"Beth, your house is beautiful. It is all that anyone could ever want or ever dream of. I am truly sorry, but I was unable to stay there because, it . . . uh . . . it made noises. Sometimes chairs would move, the stereo would go on by itself, and lights would go on. I was very scared."

Despite bearing the brunt of her anger, it was cathartic to share all that had happened at her house.

"Are you saying that my house is uh . . . uh . . . possessed or something? Are you saying that you were spooked staying here?"

Her voice had now risen to a crescendo. I knew that our friendship was at a breaking point.

"You told me yourself your workers were freaked about by something there—and you felt a presence too."

"Oh, for—"

"I'm not saying that your house is possessed. I'm just telling you that I could not sleep there. I'm sorry. I made a commitment to you that I would stay there each day you were on vacation. I did stay overnight from Saturday until Tuesday. I did not stay in your home from Wednesday to Saturday. I was there every morning at six and left for my house around ten every night. I even took your dog to my house, so he would not have to stay the night there by himself."

"Why didn't you call and tell us that you couldn't stay here? I would have gotten my father to stay in the house," she said. Her anger had subsided.

"Beth, I made a commitment to you, and I felt that I was still holding up my end of the agreement by taking care of everything." I was close to tears. "I just didn't want to ruin your vacation and bother you. I'm truly sorry."

"Will you continue to teach here?" she asked.

"Of course," I said emphatically.

"Okay."

Then she abruptly hung up. I pulled the covers over my head, turned over, and soundly fell asleep with my Bible next to me.

—~~—

Chapter 7

Pitching and swaying, my bed shook violently, like a ship tossing at sea. I was instantly thrust awake. Fear permeated every fiber of my being and my heart raced. It was evident that I was in danger. I processed the facts: My bed was floating shakily in the room and throwing me around like a limp doll. I squeezed my eyes shut because I did not want to see what was doing this to me.

This menacing power was there to destroy me. I realized this was the very presence that was at Beth's home, and now it had invaded my home, my sanctuary, and my peace. I was fully aware that I was in mortal danger.

"Jesus!" I tried to scream. My mouth moved, but no sound came out. I tried again, and I was only able to say His name in a hoarse whisper.

Suddenly and abruptly, the shaking stopped, and the bed slammed to the ground. I lay there for a moment, trying to process what happened. *Was this a dream?* No, the bed was askew, as if my question had been heard and answered.

I jumped out of bed, throwing the comforter and sheets off. I shook as I tried to turn on the light switches. I could not catch my breath, and I grabbed my chest as if I was having a heart attack. Sitting down on the antique chair in the bedroom, I glanced in the mirror above the dresser. My face was flushed, and my eyes were wild with fear. Shakily, I made my way to the kitchen, turning on every light as I walked through the house.

I wanted to call 9-1-1 and tell someone about this sinister presence that just lifted and shook my bed, terrorizing me to the very core of my being. Instead, I grabbed a bottle of ice-cold water from the refrigerator and drank thirstily. But my hands wouldn't stop shaking. I sighed loudly, and Amy came to my side. The fur on the back of her neck was sticking up, and her tail was tucked tightly between her hind legs. She licked her lips, and I knew that she was scared too. Her appearance was a confirmation that this was not some wild nightmare but a reality that scared both of us.

I patted her and then slid down the wall to sit on the floor. She sat in my lap, and I wrapped my arms around her. Tears rolled down my face and drenched Amy's neck. I was so grateful that I had her with me. She was a fierce protector, and I knew she felt that she had let me down because she was scared too and unable to react. I comforted her as she rested her beautiful face on my neck.

I walked back to the bedroom, leaving all the lights on. The bed was crooked, so I pushed it back into place. I straightened out the comforter and the sheets. After plumping the pillows, I grabbed my Bible and climbed back into bed. Amy jumped up next to me and fell soundly asleep. I draped my arm around her and held the Bible to my chest.

Suddenly, almost palpably, I could feel calm and peace restored. My anxiety was replaced with serenity. In my feeble state of mind, I was beginning to realize that Jesus had power that was astounding. I could not pray or barely utter His name, yet He still came and conquered the demons terrorizing me. I pondered this revelation. Remarkably, I fell back into a sound and peaceful sleep, comforted by a realization that I was being protected by God Almighty.

Awakening the next morning, I heard the chirping of the birds that enjoyed perching in the magnolia tree outside my bedroom window. I rolled over and peeked outside. It was a glorious morning with a pristine blue sky dotted by puffy white clouds. My mind recalled the events of the night as if they had happened to someone else. I could not believe that a bed could move like that on its own, much less rise above the ground.

I reached for my Bible that I had put next to me on the bed. I lifted the covers and stared down past my legs, but it was not there. So, I picked up all the pillows and looked underneath and around for the elusive Bible. Clearly, it was not there. Retracing my steps, I remembered the last thing I had done last night—wrapping my arms around Amy and my Bible.

I climbed out of bed, got on my hands and knees, and searched under my bed. There it was, upside down with its pages folded and rumpled. It was as if it had been thrown under the bed. Was this further evidence that there was a demonic force at work, warring against me?

The last story I read the night before was about Gideon. He was like me, questioning and asking God for reassurance. These Bible stories I'd been reading always filled me with wonder, and I began to understand that God was the only one who could give me peace. He loved me, and His love was as tangible as a soft embrace.

Throughout my life I had tried to read the Bible, but my attempts were futile. It seemed like such a waste of time, and there were times I laughed at the idea that a man, Jesus, could walk on water. Now, these stories held new meaning for me. I had seen firsthand the way God would use my prayers along with those of others to teach me that life was not what I saw with my natural eyes, but what I could not see—that there was a force, a power, that could lead me to complete peace in a sea of chaos.

This antiquated book was also filled with the sordid contents of any raunchy novel: murder, greed, manipulation, hatred, love, affairs, suspense, and irony. This book, the Bible, was very current and interesting. I loved reading my Bible. Every moment of my spare time in the days that followed, I spent reading it, meditating on it, and absorbing it.

God began to teach me lessons. The first lesson I learned was that I was meditating on the wrong message. It began with my music. I no longer could listen to my classic rock station. Instead, I sought out contemporary Christian music. Like the Bible, this music gave me the same feelings of comfort and peace every time I listened to it. I gave my rock music CDs away and bought the most recent contemporary Christian releases.

The second lesson had to do with His plans to prosper me and inspire hope in my spirit. Despair was gradually being replaced by hope, and anger and depression by optimism, courage, faith, and an expectation that my life would be one of excitement.

The most important lesson I was learning, though, was that God's power was available to me, and it could only be found through Jesus. One night while on my knees in my bedroom praying, there was loud knocking at my door. Quickly, I jumped up and went to the door, but strangely no one was there. I checked the back door, but no one was there either.

I went back into my bedroom, got on my knees, and resumed praying when the knocking started again. Once more, I checked the doors, and the realization hit me that this was a demonic force trying to distract me from praying. This time, however, I was not going to get up as the knocking persisted. Through prayer, this force could and would be destroyed, and it was here, during this time, I learned that God's power could be unleashed against any distraction, fear, or demonic force.

"Jesus, you need to go out there and get rid of this distraction!" I said firmly.

In mid-knock, the noise suddenly ceased. I realized then that the power of Jesus was greater than anything. Now that He was in my heart, I believed I was His, so He would never leave or forsake me. This was a poignant lesson because my newfound knowledge would be vital for me to get through my first year of being a born-again Christian.

—⁓—

Chapter 8

—∾—

Before drifting off to sleep, I would often get out my Bible. The Bible, full of heroes and villains, heartache and triumph, seemed to me like a brilliant painting of colors and shapes conveying new meaning every time I picked it up. Reading the stories over again shed new insights I had not understood previously. I was like a newborn babe seeing the world as if for the first time, and I could not believe what I was seeing.

Before going to bed one night during this time, I got out my Bible and read the enthralling story of a famous leader named Gideon. God commanded Gideon to do something he felt would be impossible to do—go to war against a much stronger nation. Certain of defeat, Gideon asked God to show him a sign that he would be able to overcome this fierce and formidable enemy. Carefully, he laid a pure fleece of wool on the ground. He looked to heaven and asked God to make the fleece heavily laden with dew the next morning. Surely accomplishing this impossible feat would underscore God's promise that He would be able to defeat his enemy.

The next day, Gideon anxiously came out of his tent to see the fleece saturated with water, while the ground was dry and parched. He gazed up to heaven, thanking God for this sign, and then he did the unthinkable: he began to doubt and mistrust God despite receiving the unmistakable confirmation less than a few hours before. Apprehensive and anxious, he again pleaded to God to show him another sign.

The next night, he asked God to make the drenched fleece dry and pure and the ground around it saturated with dew. He wanted to believe that with this sign from God, he would be able to do what he felt would be impossible—defeat the unbeaten enemy. The next day, Gideon awoke to the sounds of surprise and incredulity as his warriors exclaimed about the fleece that was as dry as the wings of a dove, even though it lay in a shallow pool of dew.

God had given him the sign he desired. Finding courage in God's miraculous acts, Gideon not only was able to defeat the enemy, but he also witnessed God's extraordinary hand at work, which brought him from doubt to faith.

I must admit I was a little skeptical when I read this fabulous story. How could this previously self-doubting mortal fight an enemy that no one thus far had been able to defeat? This thought settled in my mind like a cold stone, and with all my cynicism and doubt, I couldn't let it go. I slept fitfully that night, wrestling in my mind with how I would be able to know the wonderful and awesome God that I now chose to serve.

That morning, I awoke to the gentle breeze of a cool fall day. I had a lot to do before I rushed off to teach riding lessons at Beth's farm. Always the multi-tasker, I carried a basket of laundry into the kitchen and set the tea kettle on the burner to make tea.

Amy began to bark furiously in the den, which was attached to the kitchen. She spun and twirled. This was uncharacteristic of my lazy Lab. Barking was only reserved for the worst of offenses, and in her world, there were few. Today, however, she would not stop barking, and I was alarmed. As I walked into the den, I saw her crouching and snarling. She was circling a large pool of water on the carpet. It was six feet in diameter, and the water was so deep that it floated above the carpet.

I quickly grabbed towels and began to soak up the water. Amy, sensing that she was not in danger, began to sniff and paw at the ground as if she were trying to help me. I hopped on one foot with three towels underneath, but the water would not absorb into the towels. It seemed that the more I mopped and fretted, the wetter it became. In frustration, I cried out to God.

"Please God, You need to help me get rid of this water. It is not of You, so it needs to get out of here. Please God, help me!"

Then I walked around the pool, pretending that it did not bother me. I had twenty lessons to teach and two loads of wash to do, so I had no time to waste on this foolish body of water.

The dark, damp pool lay on the carpet in the den like a cancerous sore. Although I tried to ignore it, its constancy became unbearable. Each time I walked by it, I inwardly groaned.

By the third day, the ugly damp spot began to dry and was replaced with the foulest of odors. The stench was so bad that anyone who came over would think a dead body was buried there. Again, I did what I was learning to do: pray about everything.

"Please, God, get rid of this smell," I beseeched Him.

Another lesson I was learning was that God did not always give me the answer I desired. The smell lingered for days, and I suffered from the stiff, cool October breezes as I opened all the windows in my house. Gradually, the smell dissipated and became a memory I never wanted to revisit.

God was teaching me, as with Gideon, that this was a war that would not be fought by my strength—but by His. When I trusted God, and prayed to get rid of these demonic forces, He would step in. If I tried to solve a dilemma in my humanness, I soon realized that it was futile. Victory could only be attained by God—everything else was fruitless and ineffectual.

I began to realize that God was in control of everything. Prior to asking Jesus to be my Savior, I believed I was the ruler over my destiny, but this revelation turned my thinking around. No longer did I have to find a solution because God already had one for me. For the first time in my life, I wasn't walking alone but with my friend, helper, and protector—Jesus Christ. Although in my past I had mocked Him and used His name in vain, now I was becoming His biggest admirer.

My life was dramatically changing. If I ever broached the subject of what was happening in my life, people would change the subject or excuse themselves altogether. Even Sharon and Sue were getting increasingly uncomfortable talking about what was going on. And, of course, Beth was making herself scarce. I was bewildered and perplexed. A lover of people and conversation, I felt a deep loneliness covering my life like the damp fleece of Gideon's life.

These occurrences served the purpose of my Lord and Savior, whereby I was learning to lean on Him. In fact, soon He became the most important one in my life. I realized that the only one I could talk to was God, which solidified my relationship with Him. I discovered I could freely talk to Him about everything.

Coming from a stuffy and traditional religious background, I had been taught that prayer was only achieved with soft organ music in the background and a bowed head with clasped hands. I was relieved to find that I could converse with Him while my eyes were open.

At times, I was so overcome with emotion that I even cried. Spontaneously, I've broken out in praise while in deep prayer. While riding my horse, I was often overcome with emotions that I had never experienced before. I was struck by the awesomeness of God and His all-encompassing love for me.

Continual reading of the Bible allowed me to glean pertinent information about the spiritual realm I had never known. It seemed that these malevolent forces had one goal in mind—to destroy me. I clung to the verse that reassured me I was not alone nor ever would be: "He who is in me is greater than he who is in the world."

Each day I grew in my knowledge of that which was greater than the world, God Almighty. God was manifesting in my life, and without a doubt, I knew God was real. He gave me a sense of peace in a violent and scary world. He comforted me while I dwelled in fear and darkness, and He showed me His great love in my deepest moments of doubt. And there were some of those faith-shaking moments to come.

Chapter 9

T he cool, crisp air wafted across the back of my house as I hung my riding britches out to dry on the clothesline. My favorite month of the year is October. I look forward to it for several reasons. The first reason is the annoying flies and mosquitoes die. Second, I enjoy riding my horse through the gorgeous trails of my hometown in the Brandywine Valley.

This area is a national park with rolling hills, the Brandywine River, and groomed trails for the horse enthusiast. I love the brilliant oranges, reds, and golden colors of the fall foliage, and I often take pictures of this gorgeous landscape astride Raise Your Dreams. I get to meet up with friends who enjoy trail riding as much as I do. Fall is the time to get the last rides in before the horrendous Northeastern winters halt all trail riding.

I drove to work on that cool October day as the sun filled the sky. Part of my transformation as a born-again Christian meant that I no longer listened to music in the car but to sermons I found on the local Christian radio stations. That morning I listened to the tail end of one preacher's message about the importance of prayer. The next pastor came on. He was my favorite because not only were his messages poignant and thought-provoking, but he also told funny, endearing anecdotes about his life, which always illustrated his points fully. His message was about prayer too. I wondered, *Is God teaching me something?*

"In everything, and at every opportunity, pray," the pastor said. "Ask God for protection. Remember, the devil is like a lion ready to devour, destroy, and kill. Don't ever leave anything to chance."

He continued with a story about how he forgot to pray about an upcoming mini-vacation with his family. Comically, the car had a flat tire in the middle of the trip, the dog threw up in the back seat, and the luggage on top of the station wagon fell off en- route to their destination. He shared that because even though he was looking forward to fun, it was nothing but stressful trying to find the luggage, straighten out the tire, and get the dog to the vet. He realized that prayers should be spoken before every activity because if you don't pray, you let your guard down and leave yourself open to attack.

I was learning that if God wants you to learn or understand something, He will repeat the message, sermon, or story. This is not unlike the Bible, in which the first four books of the New Testament are the same. Although they offer different perspectives, they deliver the same message.

Was this a warning of something to come? I decided to do exactly what the pastor was preaching. I turned off the radio and focused my attention on praying.

"God, I'm not sure what I'm supposed to pray for specifically, but please protect me and keep me safe."

It was a lame prayer. And with only a mile left in my drive, I knew that once I got to school, I wouldn't have a moment to myself to be able to pray. I had to convince myself that those few words would do the job. But would they?

The day buzzed along. After teaching school, I anticipated a riding lesson with a German Olympian. Richard, an Olympic coach for Austria, was visiting this area of the country. The best riders in the northeastern corridor of the United States would be meeting with him, and I was fortunate enough to schedule a lesson with this talented man.

He agreed to travel to Beth's barn where I kept my horse. My students were eager to see their instructor (me) receive a healthy dose of humble pie.

As I got out of my car, I was greeted by a few of my students. They had gotten my horse out of the paddock and had him groomed so beautifully that his feet sparkled with toe polish. I was grateful because I only had a half hour to get him warmed up and ready for what I anticipated would be one of the best experiences of my life.

As Richard walked into the indoor riding ring, there was an audible gasp. He was wearing custom-made black riding boots with full-seat deer-skin breeches, a vest, and a small European cap on his head. In his left hand, he held a long dressage whip, and in his right a pair of white supple leather gloves. There was not a hair out of place. He was a picture of health, vigor, and strength.

"Hello, Jill," he said with a heavy German accent. He walked over to my horse and patted him with his broad hands while he inspected my tack.

"It is good to see you, Mr. Uhlmann," I said, and I really meant it. It seemed that everyone was captivated by this wonderful man. He had trained the best of the best, and to think that he would teach me was almost too much to grasp.

As the lesson progressed, he pushed me to new heights of understanding, explaining the progression and movements of the horse, while clarifying what aids I would have to employ to achieve these difficult movements. Within a few moves, my horse was doing tempi changes, cantering in different leads. Not only was I impressed with what my horse was doing, but Richard was dumbfounded. I knew he only worked with talented European Warmbloods.

"Jill, this is unbelievable! Dis horse cannot do dis. He do dis because he loves you."

He stood there with whip in hand, gently tapping it into his other hand as if he were clapping. Clearly, he was perplexed yet impressed.

My students, who had been sitting quietly in the observation section, broke out into loud applause. Richard looked over at his audience and started to laugh. Always a teacher, he walked over and began to explain why my horse could not do what I was asking of him. According to Richard, my horse did not have the correct confirmation or athletic talent required to complete the movement.

Richard said he saw a hunger and a desire in me, as well as a remarkable relationship between my horse and me. As the lesson wound down, he commented, "Jill, I travel all over da world. You have an unbelievable relationship with dis horse. I never seen it before." He patted Raise Your Dreams' broad shoulder. "I want to work wit you again!"

We quickly set up another date, and I was thrilled. After putting my horse into his stall with a bowl full of peeled and sliced apples, his absolute favorite treat, I stood outside of his stall like a proud mother. Everyone, including Beth, was congratulating me and giving my horse accolades, which he seemed to enjoy as much as I did.

I drove home that day as the sun began to set, filled with thanksgiving because I realized that God was giving me the desires of my heart. My horse had won over the hearts and minds of my students, as well as this highly esteemed riding instructor and trainer from Europe.

That night I took a long, hot shower, savoring every word that Richard spoke, especially about the special relationship that my horse and I had. I got into bed, and Amy, not enjoying the sudden temperature drop, curled under the blankets and rested her head on the pillow next to mine.

But I loved the cooler temperatures and grabbed another comforter from the closet and put it on my bed. Amy shuddered to confirm that she was cold and needed another blanket. I tucked her in like a child and chuckled. What an extraordinary day it had been, and cuddling up with Amy, my fuzzy bundle of fluff, was the perfect way to end it.

I grabbed the Bible from the nightstand, along with a notebook that I used to write down verses that seemed to have the same theme. I often searched for Bible verses teaching on the same topic. I happened to be studying what the Bible had to say about protection. Every time I came across a verse about protection, I wrote it down. I had collected quite a few and was impressed that even though I had only read a few books of the Bible, I had accrued quite a collection of verses on topics that were important to me.

After reading Psalm 23, I wrote this verse in my journal: "Even though I walk through the shadow of death, I will fear no evil, for you are with me; your rod and your staff, they comfort me." I put my pen in my mouth and began to scan through the Bible, resting on Psalm 46:1, "God is our refuge and strength, a very present help in trouble."

I wrote the verse down and closed the journal. I began to fight my drooping eyelids. Suddenly, my day had caught up with me, and I became very tired. I quickly glanced at the clock and noticed it was already after nine.

I reached over and put my Bible and journal on the nightstand and turned off the light. Amy sighed as if she had been waiting all day for this moment, to sleep in my downy bed with the only person she loves—me.

"God, thank You for this day and the opportunity to ride my horse in a lesson with Richard," I softly said. "You're my help and refuge. Amen." I closed my eyes and rolled over to face Amy.

No sooner had I fallen asleep when I was suddenly awakened from a sound sleep by the tearing of my flesh. My back was being ripped open. I could almost hear the maniacal laugh of some hideous being. The smell of rotting flesh permeated the room. I could feel blood seeping through my T-shirt.

"Oh my God, what is going on?" I screamed out loud.

I threw the comforters off the bed. Amy jumped off, with her tail between her legs, while she followed closely behind me to the bathroom.

I turned on the bathroom light and pulled off my shirt to confirm what I felt. Three long traces of blood had seeped through my shirt. I grabbed my makeup mirror and glanced in the vanity at my naked back. Six-inch long gashes starting at the base of my neck to the middle of my back were like a highway of blood.

I could feel a malevolent presence in the room. Its clammy claws grabbed at my ankles, and fear paralyzed my body. Breathing became hard and my heart raced. I was frightened to the core of my being.

"Jesus, help me!" I called out. Then I quoted the verse that I had just read and written in my journal only a few hours before: "God, You are my refuge and strength, a very present help in trouble. I am in trouble! Please send help and keep me safe." The icy grip at my ankles fell away, and I suddenly felt peace washing away my fear and anxiety.

I grabbed rubbing alcohol off the shelf and dabbed it on the now bleeding and pulsating red wounds. I winced in pain because moving was torment. Each move was met with stinging agony. I immediately thought of the torture that Jesus endured before He was hung on the cross. Forty lashes He withstood. Yet I could barely tolerate three tiny scrapes compared to His terrible wounds.

I could not reach my back to put on bandages, so I put on three T-shirts and carefully crawled back into bed, trying not to lie on my back. Amy jumped up next to me, and I involuntarily moaned. Remarkably, I fell asleep right away.

The alarm blared in the distance, and I groggily got up. I was reminded of the attack from the night before as the pain from my wounds reared its ugly head. The movement out of the bed re-opened the scabs, and the bleeding started anew. I cringed in pain, carefully pulling my shirts up and over the wounds. I glanced in the mirror at the three deep gashes down my back. I put on a light pink turtleneck to hide them. I did not want students or the school staff to see these wounds, which came from something not of this world.

I was eager to get to school and show Sharon. When I got to school, I went into Sharon's nurse's office. She was sitting at her desk going over paperwork. It was too early for any students to be in the building, but I still closed the door behind me.

"Sharon, you are not going to believe what happened last night," I said as I pulled down my turtleneck away from the back of my neck.

She grabbed her glasses and stood behind me, gingerly pulling my turtleneck down. "What on earth?" she said.

"I know, I got scratched last night."

"How far down do they go?"

I pulled my shirt up.

"Oh my, this is awful. They are deep. What on earth did this?" She readjusted my shirt.

"Demons!" I was as shocked as she was with my curt answer.

"Why?" she asked.

"I don't know. Ironically, the last thing I read in the Bible before I went to bed was a passage about protection. After this happened, I recalled from memory verses that spoke about protection. Immediately, I got up and surveyed these marks when I could feel something clawing at my leg."

"This is weird. Let's go talk to Mike," she said, pulling me out of the room.

Mike was a science teacher. He was steadfast and resolute in his faith. Like Sue, he was a leader in the Christian community and rock solid in his faith. After I got saved, the small Christian-teacher community at school embraced me and we formed an informal group of teachers who would pray for each other and share our needs each morning in Mike's room. This group was comprised of Sharon, Sue, Mike, Sylvia, and me.

We wended our way now through a labyrinth of halls to the science wing. Mike's room was illuminated, and we could see him putting out microscopes on each student's desk. We startled him as we opened his door.

"Good morning, Sharon and Jill. What brings the two of you down here?" he asked.

"Check this out. Jill has something on her back." Sharon twirled me around to put my back toward him.

Sharon pulled down my turtleneck to reveal the deep gashes. While he studied the marks, I explained what had happened the night before.

"Jill, I'm not an expert in this. I have never heard of this nor has anyone that I know ever experienced this before. I am concerned about this, though. You are in danger and need protection." He leaned forward, walking his hands across the desk. "I'm calling my church leaders to pray specifically for you. Let's get the prayer group together this afternoon and pray for you before you leave school. Do you ever quote Scripture before you go to bed?"

"No, I don't exactly know what you mean," I said.

"Don't worry," he said. "Meet me after school in my room, and I will show you how to do it."

The day was marked by turmoil: a serious fight erupted in the hall, a student in my class broke down and cried because her boyfriend broke up with her, and another student told me that his mother threatened to kick him out of her home. I was not only exhausted mentally but physically as well. Throughout the day, I was constantly reminded of the trauma of the three scratches. Every movement seemed to be attached to my back, and the wounds kept bleeding.

Finally, the bell rang, signaling the end of the day, and I could hardly make my way to the science wing to see Mike. He was waiting for me. In front of him was his three-hundred-pound black leather Bible. He was writing on a piece of paper verses from the Bible, which he was thumbing through at a frantic pace.

Everyone else had assembled. As they peered at the raw, red, and pulsing cuts down my back, everyone was solemn and aghast. Some in the group were charismatics, and others were fundamentalists, but everyone believed that God could protect each of us—even from unseen, brutal forces such as these.

"We are gathered here to pray for Jill," Mike began. "And we need to keep her in prayer. Although all of us know that the devil and his cohorts can wreak havoc, it seems that they are revealing the tangible results of being in danger. Jill will probably have the scars to prove it. I want to show her how to pray using Scripture, the most powerful tool of all, to protect and provide."

There were nods. Some whispered, "Yes, Jesus." Almost everyone scooted forward in their seats.

"Jill, all you need to do is find the Scripture that applies to your situation and then bring it into your prayer. For example, my favorite Scripture is Psalm 91. When I am in trouble or need help, this is my go-to Scripture."

He took a deep breath, bowed his head, and closed his eyes. We all followed his lead. My heart was hammering.

"Father God, You are the Almighty, Wonderful Counselor, and lover of my soul. Your Word says that You will deliver us from the snare of the fowler and the deadly pestilence. Jill needs Your protection from the snare and pestilence. Protect and guide her. She will not be afraid of the terror by night. You will cover her with Your wings. She shall not be afraid. We ask it in Jesus' name," he concluded, opening his eyes.

I wanted to clap because the prayer made my heart soar with happiness. I pretended that I was pushing my hair out of my eyes because

I could feel tears begin to form. I was always that way with Scripture— it made me want to cry, especially when it dealt specifically with the situation that I was facing.

"Wow, that is amazing!" I said.

"Here are some verses that I copied down during my lunch period that I think we need to pray over you. I made a few copies for all of us."

He gave us each two pages of verses in his tiny script—words plucked from the Bible. I was moved and amazed that someone would do something like that for me.

"Thanks, Mike. I am touched by what you did for me."

"No problem!" he said.

We all got into a small circle and began to pray. I had many friends but none who had ever given up their lunch period for me. Being a Christian had many perks, and one of them was having friends who truly cared. They said they just wanted to build me up through encouraging Scripture. What I realized was that God revealed the largest key to knowing Him, and it involved repeating His words of hope and peace.

That night, my journal gained forty more verses, and I imagined a host of angels surrounding me to protect me and destroy my enemy. I never slept so soundly in my life.

—∿∿—

Chapter 10

―⁓―

It was a brutally cold and blustery night, not long after the gashes appeared. I was teaching in Beth's indoor riding ring. Many of my students were determined to ride in the wind chill, even though the temperature was only in the single digits and low teens. By the fourth lesson, I was losing all feeling in my feet, and my breath came out in a steady stream of steam.

My last student of the night was Karen, a woman in her fifties who had learned to sacrifice for her children and put their needs and desires before her own. Now that they had all grown up and were pursuing their own dreams, she had decided to pursue hers, which included learning how to ride a horse.

Karen was a joy to teach. She asked interesting and thoughtful questions that showed she was not only learning this sport but becoming a great horsewoman as well. She absorbed each lesson and painstakingly worked on commanding her body to contort itself into positions that she had never been asked to do, such as two-point, heels down, and posting using her hips. She loved riding, and she formed relationships with each of the lesson horses.

She prepared herself for each lesson by cutting up chunks of carrots and apples. She also peeled them, not wanting the horses or ponies to bite into a hard or dirty chunk. Also saving the stringy tops of the carrots, she enjoyed watching the horses gingerly navigating their way around them. She always had peppermint candies in her pocket too, as well as a small plastic bag of Cheerios. She giggled unashamedly every time the horses nuzzled her neck and moved their lips across her pants pockets searching for the elusive treats.

That night she came into the ring like she always did, decked out in the best riding attire that money could buy. She was wearing dark brown riding britches with suede patches, tall dress boots freshly polished, a brand-new matching sweater and vest, a deep-red riding jacket, and a jet-black helmet, along with her fine deerskin leather gloves. Her makeup was fresh, and her bright pink lipstick complemented her subtle pink turtleneck.

I won't deny that I was jealous. I worked full time as a high school teacher, and after a long arduous day at school, I either went to Beth's farm and taught riding lessons or rode Raise Your Dreams. By this time in the evening, my mascara was smudged so it looked like I had dark circles under my eyes, dirt was caked under my nails, my boots were full of mud, and my britches were christened with slobber from the horses. Tiny hairs from the horses adorned my jacket like a fuzzy sweater. In contrast to me, Karen was like a breath of fresh air. As her perfume wafted across my nose, I deeply breathed in its sweet citrus scent.

When I told her that she would be riding her favorite mount, Napoleon, she clasped her hands in glee and started to laugh. Most people did not like the old, cantankerous gelding. But for her, he would do almost anything. She understood that sometimes it just takes forming a relationship with horses to truly see the gem that each horse held inside. She had learned all his ticklish spots and his favorite treats, peppermint candies. She had also discovered that after his saddle was taken off, he loved his girth area scratched with her perfectly manicured nails. In thanks, he wrapped his big block head around her shoulder, and they stayed that way until she kissed him on his soft, downy muzzle.

It was almost impossible to get him to the mounting block, but she had learned what few had taken the time to understand—that Napoleon could not refuse peppermint candies. All she had to do was crinkle the cellophane wrapper, and he followed her like an obedient puppy to the block.

"My God, Jill, I can't feel my feet. This is not a good sign!" she said as she started to walk to the mounting block that evening. Karen was not a complainer, but I was concerned that she was this cold before she had even gotten on her horse.

"No, Karen, I don't think it is either. Hopefully, when you get warmed up, you won't feel so cold. If you need to cut the lesson short, I will understand. It *is* very cold."

I secretly hoped she would want to leave early. My feet were so numb that I could not feel the ground, so I was bordering on misery myself.

"What! Leave early?! I savor every moment I'm riding Napoleon, and I would rather freeze to death than not ride!" She patted her patient mount on the shoulder as she swung up into the saddle. Reaching into her pocket, she brought out a peppermint, which Napoleon turned his head to reach with his lips. This was further evidence that this horse would do anything for her, and I knew without a doubt that she would do anything for him.

"Hey, Karen, I know this sounds crazy, but let's pray about this cold. I bet if we ask God to warm us up, He will," I said.

I knew it was crazy to think like this, but I felt that if I prayed about something, God would answer my prayers. After all, I had enough evidence.

This was the first time I shared with someone that God could do what seemed impossible. I thought Karen would laugh. Instead, she looked intently into my face. I knew Karen had left her husband of thirty years and was now living with her boyfriend. Her language and conversation led me to believe that she did not have much faith in God—or in anyone else, for that matter.

"What do you mean? Pray to God that He will keep us warm?" Then she shrugged and paused as if in deep thought. "Well, what do we have to lose?" She chuckled, and I did, too.

I walked over to her and put my hand on her horse, and she grabbed my other hand. It became very quiet and still. She bowed her head, and I bowed mine. This would be a first, praying with confidence in front of a virtual stranger.

"Lord, could You make us warm? It is freezing, and I have been out here for over four hours. Please, Lord, make us warm. Thank You! Amen."

She squeezed my hand and I laughed.

As soon as I stepped back, it felt as if a warm liquid was being poured over my head, down over my shoulders, and back, flowing through my legs and seeping deep into my feet and toes. My whole body began to perspire. My face flushed in excitement. I started to grin as I unzipped my jacket. I opened my mouth to speak, but all I could do was laugh.

Karen started to laugh too. "Jill, this is incredible! I am actually hot. It feels like warm water is being poured over me. Is this happening to you too?"

"Yeah, this is unreal!" I said.

I couldn't believe it. God had showed up in our circumstances and changed a situation that should have been unchangeable.

"Jill, you must have some power. You asked for warmth and He provided it. How did you do that?"

"I didn't do it! God did it!" I laughed.

Karen was the first person with whom I shared the gospel, the good news message. My eyes filled with tears, and I told her that God had been tugging on my heart for a while now. The moment I asked Jesus into my heart, my life changed forever.

"Well, I want what you have!" Karen said.

"You can. Just ask Jesus into your heart."

"How?" She held up her hands.

"Easy!" I said. I led her in the prayer that Pastor Don had said to me on September 1, 1995, at seven in the morning.

"Heavenly Father, I know that I am a sinner. I ask that you wash away my sins through the blood of Jesus. Come dwell in my heart, Jesus, and be with me forever."

Karen repeated after me. Her eyes welled up as she flung her leg around Napoleon and leaped off him with grace. She hugged me hard for what seemed like minutes.

"Jill, I not only saw God answer your prayer earlier tonight, but now I feel different—lighter. I came for a riding lesson, but what I got was far better. Thank you!" Tears spilled over her lower lids.

"Karen, you are now born again," I said. "You will see how much God loves you. He will show you every day."

As I drove home that night, I kept thinking about the power available to me through prayer. The night was emotional because it was the first time I had shared with another person what Pastor Don had shared with me just a few months before.

This was only a precursor to what God had planned for my life. This was the start of a special journey that would take me through devastating heartbreak as well as soaring triumphs and successes. My life as I had known it was being altered, and the sharp, jagged pieces were being softened and fitted back together into a glorious existence.

—*∽*—

Chapter 11

—⁓—

Everything was changing. It was evident in the way I taught in the classroom, the way I instructed riding students at the farm, what I watched on TV, and how I spent my free time. I was becoming a "new" person, with ideas, beliefs, and a mindset that were foreign to me. I was being born anew.

My friends noticed the change. No longer was I interested in going to the latest bar or club looking for a man to help me escape the trials of my life. I comprehended for the first time that my foundation was built on an immovable rock that promised to never leave or forsake me. The elusive unconditional love was always there, living inside me.

The biggest change came in the classroom. I found myself offering hope to my disheartened and depressed students. The hope I had was permanent and lasting. My students were drawn to me and my new belief system. Although I could not initiate a conversation about Jesus or my faith, they constantly sought to understand my beliefs. They could sense the peace that permeated my being, along with the genuine love and respect I had towards them. Jesus was operating through me, and I found that the least lovable students were the ones I loved the most.

Some would stay after school, helping me to run errands, clean up, or just sit and talk. One student was a very troubled young man named Burt. He had bright red hair and a small, scrawny body, and his high-pitched whine grated on everyone's nerves.

"Miss Dorsey, may I ask you a question?" he asked one day. I could sense in his troubled eyes that he needed reassurance about something that was clearly bothering him.

"Sure, Burt. What's up?" I said.

I sat down at a student's desk, and he sat across from me. He slumped in the desk and alternated between wringing his hands and doodling in his notebook.

I waited for a response, and it seemed that he had a hard time looking me in the eye.

"What religion are you?" he finally asked.

I explained that my faith was not based on a religion but on a relationship with Jesus Christ.

"I would like to have a relationship with Jesus Christ. How do I get one?" he asked, as his voice caught in his throat.

Even though I had shared with friends and family how to become a born-again Christian, this was the first time I would explain it to a student. I said that being "born again" was a condition of the heart. It could only come from first recognizing that we are all sinners. When Jesus took on our sins the day He died on the cross, He made a way for all to go to heaven. He bore our deserved punishment.

His eyes brimmed with tears. He bowed his head and asked if I could help him ask Jesus into his life.

I began, "Dear Father . . ."

Suddenly, he stood up, upsetting the desk, his face full of rage and torment.

"What are you doing? You cannot pray with me!" he screamed. He stood there pointing his finger at me and spitting out the words with venom.

He stomped to the door and slammed it so hard that the phone on the wall fell out of its cradle.

I was taken aback. It was as if I had been pummeled, and I felt my heart racing. I walked to the phone and put it back up and then straightened out the desks. Picking up my book bag, I grabbed my purse from the drawer. I locked my door and walked outside on the beautiful spring day. Although I could hear the track coach yelling out drills and the girls practicing cheers in anticipation of cheerleading try-outs, I walked out among them dejectedly with a heavy heart.

Driving home, I felt my chest constricting. I could not catch my breath, nor could I pray. Once I got home, I went straight to my bedroom, pulled my now well-worn Bible off the nightstand, and knelt at the edge of the bed with it clutched tightly against my chest.

"Lord, I'm going to lose my job," I said, "this boy has set me up. I'm going to get fired. I did try to pray with him on school property. Please, Lord, I need Your word."

The desperation I felt was palpable. Amy nudged my hand as I opened the Bible.

It automatically opened to Psalm 91. I read it out loud, and then I started to cry. I could not believe the words.

I will say of the Lord,

He is my refuge and my fortress; my God in Him I will trust.

Surely He will deliver you from the snare of the fowler.....

He shall cover you with His feathers and under His wings you shall take refuge; His truth shall be your shield and buckler...

No evil shall befall you....

for He shall give His angels charge over you to keep you in all of your ways......

Because he has set his love upon Me, therefore I will deliver him;

I will set him on high, because he has known My name.....

With long life I will satisfy him.

That night I slept fitfully, one moment trusting God and His Word and the next allowing fear and foreboding to overwhelm my active imagination. Throughout the night, I flicked on my light, grabbed my Bible, and read Psalm 91 over again. It gave me peace and allowed me to wrap myself in a love I had never known before.

I felt as if I had just closed my eyes when the earsplitting sound of my alarm beckoned me to tackle a challenge I was not ready to handle. In my mind I saw before me the police, the school administrators, the school board president, and Burt with his parents. My imagination was working overtime, and I needed to check my new reality, the glorious Word of God. I pulled open my Bible to Psalm 91 and read word for word out loud how He would guide and protect me.

"God, you cannot go back on Your Word, right?" I said aloud. I hoped I would receive an audible response, but instead I was swathed in a peace that was not of this world.

I drove to school in a daze. Once I got there, I prayed one last prayer before going into what I felt was the lion's den. The front office was encased in glass, so I could see the interior office. My principal was leaning on the counter, laughing and joking with a science teacher who loved to tell jokes. There were no police, nor Burt or anyone else.

Bolstered by this revelation, I grabbed the cold, metallic door knob and threw open the door, loudly proclaiming, "Good morning!" Then I grabbed my folder from my mailbox.

"Good morning, Jill," they all responded and went back to their conversations.

"Hey, Jill." My heart skipped a billion beats as my principal said, "Have a great day!"

"You too!" was all I could respond.

After unlocking the door to my classroom, I checked to make sure nothing was amiss. My books were still haphazardly piled in my bookcase. There were still unmarked papers on my desk, and the desk that Burt had sat in was in perfect order. I started to tidy up the desks and get paper and pencils out for my first period of the day when suddenly the door opened.

It was Burt, his whole five feet four inches standing in the doorway. His eyes were wild and red, as if he had been crying.

I stood there transfixed. He was eerily unpredictable, so I was fearful. My heart was pounding so fast that I thought it would surely burst.

He moved into the classroom, but I stopped him by walking toward him. I did not need a repeat of him slamming my door and overturning the desk.

"Miss Dorsey, I'm sorry about yesterday. I want you to know that I went home and thought about what you said. I've decided to ask Jesus into my heart. You're right, it changes you! Hey, it was the first night I've slept through the night in two weeks. Thank you for telling me how to get saved. Have a great day!"

He said it all so fast that I did not have time to digest it all.

Before I could say anything, he literally leapt out of the room. I slumped into the desk because my knees were buckling. This was an outcome I could not have expected or foreseen.

From that time forth, Burt continued to stop by my classroom after school and ask me questions about the Bible and his relationship with Jesus Christ. It drove me closer in my relationship with Jesus as well because I had to teach it to this boy, who was becoming a fine young man.

He became serious about not only studying the Bible but studying his school work as well. He went from barely getting by as a D- student to becoming an A+ student. He now had his eyes on a goal that he thought would be something he could love—a career as a nurse. As he got ready for graduation that year, his visits became so frequent that when he failed to show up one day, I was concerned.

The next morning, he stopped by to tell me that he was dealing with some awful "stuff" at home. I told him that God would see him through any trial.

Then he slumped in the desk and said, "My mom is gay! Yup, she moved her girlfriend in last night! She is very pretty and not dikey at all. My mom told me to tell people that she is my aunt, but I can't lie. I can't believe my mom is a lesbian. She makes fun of me reading the Bible and my faith. It's really hard, Miss Dorsey." And with that, tears began to roll down his face.

I walked over and gave him a tissue, but he was inconsolable. I realized that I did not have any answers, nor could I because only God could see him through this trial too.

I learned that being a Christian was hard, as it could jeopardize job security and put one in compromising positions. My belief system expanded, however, with the knowledge that "with God all things are possible" (Matthew 19:26).

Like a bricklayer, Jesus was slowly building one principle upon another in my mind. The more I sought Jesus, the more I became like Him. I learned to hear His voice and understand His teaching. The year was hard and trying, but it taught me how to hold onto faith. Little did I know that within a few months, my faith would be tested even more because I would be asked to give up what I loved the most.

———~~~———

Chapter 12

～～～

"Please come a little early. I would like to speak with you," my mother said. We were talking on the phone about our plans for Thanksgiving, which was always at my parents' luxurious home in Delaware.

"Is there something the matter?" I asked. I knew that something was bothering my mother. She was never reticent in letting her children know when they disappointed her.

"We'll talk about it before Thanksgiving dinner," she said firmly.

Before I could respond, she had already hung up the phone. Clearly, she did not want to speak about it before then.

I sat on the couch and went through everything that I thought could get my mom mad. Nothing came to mind. I spent the next day trying to forget the angry tone of her voice, along with the dread that was now hovering over one of my favorite holidays.

I went into the spare bedroom that evening and stripped the sheets. I was going to have a little visitor over the extended weekend—my ten-year-old nephew, Jason. Jason was the product of a destructive relationship that my sister had with her high school sweetheart. The father was in and out of jail, and Jody was on a slippery slide of self-annihilation, which included a stint in California. Unfortunately, Jason came back not only much thinner but had also lost his ability to speak. He was filthy, and his drooping diaper showed that he had been uncared for while he had been away with his mother in California.

My sister no longer wanted to be saddled with the responsibility of raising a child when she could not even take care of herself. She called me three days before school started earlier that year and asked if I would take Jason. I explained that I could not do that with only three days to find a day care and set up a home for him. She was disappointed and hung up on me. My parents had already been letting Jody and Jason live at their home since they felt it best to keep him in a stable home. Gradually, his speech came back, and my mom enrolled him in a special school. Although he was developmentally delayed, it was not because he was lacking intelligence.

He was a beautiful child with big brown eyes flecked with gold and green. He had shockingly white-blonde hair that framed a round face with pink pouty lips he liked to pucker together when he was thinking. Jason was reckless. By the time he was eight years old, he had been hit by a car and bitten by the neighbor's dog, sprained his collar bone, broke his pinky, and had surgery on his back. Through it all, he had never complained or made excuses. He was always full of fun and surprises.

I had a full weekend planned for the little guy. I would take him to my house after Thanksgiving dinner. We would make popcorn, which he loved, and watch his favorite Veggie Tales movie. On Friday, we would wake up early and hike out to the reservoir and throw balls to Amy. Then we would stop at his favorite restaurant in the whole world, Chuck E. Cheese's. I promised him ten dollars to play arcade games.

Then on Sunday we would go to church and invite my neighbors' kids to come over for pizza. He loved the neighborhood kids, and the park was where they built forts, rode bikes, and on one occasion caught a snake that they put in a shoe box and kept on my kitchen table.

I put on his favorite sheets, the periwinkle blue "fuzzy" ones. They were made from soft cotton jersey material. He had picked out these sheets while shopping in the mall one afternoon with me. I was always careful to put them on his bed when he came over, which was almost every weekend. I liked to give my parents a break from the always inquisitive little ten-year-old.

The night before Thanksgiving, I prayed for peace and asked God to help me understand my mother's point of view. The next morning, I awoke to flurries. Amy was excited, and she jumped up and down in anticipation of snow. I grabbed my exercise gear, and we started a slow jog up to the park. By the time we got to the "doggy field," I was sopping with sweat. Amy flew from one dog to another, eager to greet each one. I laughed and told the dog owners that she was running for a political office.

We left the park, and I ate a sparse breakfast before I took a shower. I dressed casually because my family is informal. I wore my favorite sweater from Ireland with the fur-lined hood and side pockets with a zipper. I slipped into jeans and boots and grabbed Amy's leash. This was her favorite holiday too. Being the only dog in the family had its perks, and she was eager to devour some of my mom's home-cooked turkey too.

Smell is the most memorable sense, and I can understand why. As soon as I opened the door, I was greeted with the aromas of cinnamon, apples, turkey, cranberries, freshly baked yeasty bread, and sweet potatoes.

My mother was in her domain. She had a gloved mitt in one hand and a spatula in the other.

"Mom, it smells delicious!" I said, leaning over the counter to kiss her. She leaned in and gave me half a cheek. I pecked her and she air-kissed me. That was the usual thing between us, so I thought nothing of it.

"What can I help you with?" I asked while I stirred the potatoes that were boiling. This was a formality because my mom hated help. I was a lot like her. We enjoyed doing things our way, and having help was sometimes a hindrance and a kink in our flow.

She shook her head and took off her apron as she turned all the burners down to simmer. She walked across the kitchen and opened the French doors to the den, indicating that this is where she would like me to go. This would be a private conversation. I followed her into the den like a dead man accepting a noose.

"Sit down," she said, motioning to the couch.

She sat across the room in an overstuffed chair. Her small body was enveloped in its cavernous cushions, and she shifted to get comfortable. Then she reached into her pants pocket and withdrew a crumpled piece of paper. It was yellow with wide lines, so I knew it came from Jason's school. It was the paper he used to practice his handwriting.

Good, I thought, *she's going to ask me a question about Jason's schooling.* I noticed that her body was rigid as she grabbed her glasses on the table in front of her.

I could make out a child's uncoordinated writing. It was a note addressed to Jason.

She started to read aloud.

Dear Jason,

I am sorry that I made you cry. I will not say bad things to you anymore.

Your friend,

Sam

What does this mean? I wondered. She slowly folded the letter into a small original square and peered over her glasses at me. Her eyes then started to fill with tears, but she composed herself.

Jason was going to a new school, one that could and would address his social and psychological issues. He had been making great progress, and it seemed that he was making friends; so, when my mom found this note, she was taken aback.

"I found this letter in Jason's book bag," she said. "When I asked Jason, what had happened that made him cry, he told me that Sam was cursing on the playground. Jason told Sam that he shouldn't curse because his Aunt Jill said that it was wrong, and God wouldn't like it. Then Sam and his friends teased Jason, and he started to cry. His teacher made Sam write a letter to Jason to apologize for teasing him."

After pausing, my mother continued, "Jill, I am tired of you talking to Jason about Jesus and God. Now he's getting teased, and he already has enough strikes against him. He doesn't need to be labeled a Jesus freak. I do not want you to take him to church. You cannot talk to him about God or Jesus. This is unacceptable, and I will not have it!" Her voice had now reached a high pitch.

I knew that my mom was looking for an outlet to thrust her frustration upon and I did not want it to be me. I had to speak around the lump in my throat.

"Mom, what you are asking me to do is impossible," I said, softly but firmly. "I cannot separate Jesus from me. He is in my heart. He permeates my every thought and action. I am really sorry, but I cannot do what you are demanding of me."

My mother was a hospital administrator, and hundreds of people were under her direct supervision; so, when she spoke, people listened. Directives from my mother were non-negotiable. Her daughter refusing to follow her orders was just too much. Her face tightened, and she took a deep breath.

"Then you can forget about taking him this weekend or any weekend, for that matter," she said resolutely. "He needs friends, not to become some weirdo or the butt of his classmates' jokes!"

"I understand your point," I said, surprised by my calm voice.

Even though I could feel my heart being broken slowly and methodically, I did not let on to my heartache. I realized that God was allowing the one and only person I loved with all my heart to be taken from me because of my dedication to Jesus. Jason was my sunshine and I was his. He was not only my little nephew, but, I thought, the only child I would ever have in my life.

I slowly walked outside. Snow flurries flew through the air. As the storm gathered in intensity, I felt an ache in my heart that was too hard to bear.

I climbed into my car. Amy followed behind and jumped into the back seat. I knew she would be confused because there would be no little boy to throw a ball to her all weekend. I started the car and drove down the driveway. As I glanced into the dining room window, I saw my mom remove my place setting.

There is a verse in the Bible about mothers going against daughters and daughters going against mothers. Jesus came into my life, and it cost me all that I loved. My mother was turning away from me, my nephew was being taken from me, and I was alone again.

Frozen pizza would have to suffice for my Thanksgiving meal. I sat at my kitchen table with the lights dimmed so no one could see how dejected I was. I flipped through the Bible, trying to find the verse that addressed the issue that to follow Jesus Christ may mean you have to leave your earthly family.

Later, I found out that Jason cried when my mother told him he was not going to my house over the Thanksgiving weekend. He loved spending time with me, as well as the kids in the neighborhood. He looked forward to walking to the park, riding his bike, and playing with Amy.

Three long months later, my mom called to ask me if I would keep Jason while she and my father went away. They wanted to visit friends and needed someone to take Jason.

"Mom, you know I'm going to talk about Jesus and God. I will take him to church. Are you going to be okay with that?" I asked.

"Yeah, do whatever you want," she said, apparently annoyed that I even asked her.

My heart soared.

The day I went to pick up Jason, he had his little book bag packed with his children's Bible I had bought for him. As he climbed into the car, he opened the Bible and told me that he had been reading about a guy who was eaten by a big fish.

We spent the night talking about how God had big plans for him—plans that would help him succeed and give him hope.

"Yeah, I know, Aunt Jill," he said.

I tussled his golden blonde hair and gave him a big kiss.

He grabbed my hand and said, "I'm glad I'm here! Can I have some popcorn?"

"Of course, little buddy!" I said. As I went into the kitchen, I felt my throat constrict because I wanted to cry. A few months ago, this would have been impossible, but it seems that with God all things are possible.

God knew my heart, and He certainly knew that I needed my nephew, who was a bundle of joy and happiness. Faithfully, God continued to show me that His love is greater than I can imagine, and He truly works everything out for my good.

<center>~~~</center>

Chapter 13

———

Little did I know that being denied time spent with Jason would only be the first of many tests and trials I would have to endure because I was a born-again Christian. Now my faith was being tested again, but in a realm, I never thought possible. Nevertheless, I wondered how I could ever say that God was my priority without truly putting Him first.

But another thing I loved was being taken away from me. My position as a riding instructor at Beth's farm was being seized and stolen from a heart that was already broken.

The phone call came late on Friday night. I usually don't answer the phone so late, but I noticed that it was Beth calling and thought that it was probably about the lessons on Saturday morning. Saturday morning was always marked by a flurry of activity. Arrive at the barn at seven and write the schedule for the day on the chalkboard, organize the students and the horses that they would be riding, and teach until five that evening. I was averaging fifteen to twenty-five students every Saturday, and it was busy—so busy that it was impossible to go to the bathroom, much less grab a bite to eat.

"Hey, Beth!" I said.

"Jill!" Beth said harshly.

"Yes?" I wondered why she was calling and seemed so upset.

"Did I get you up?" she asked, even though she was obviously unconcerned.

"No, I was just lying in bed reading," I said.

"Oh. I noticed that you have been stressed out lately. I decided that it would be best if someone took over your lessons, so you can take some time off. You know, maybe come back in the summer." Beth was blunt and to the point. This conversation was not a discussion—it was an edict. I got up and paced, phone in hand.

"Beth, I'm sorry that you have that impression, but I'm not stressed out. I love my job at your farm. I have gotten close to the students, the horses, and the helpers. It's something I look forward to every week."

"Jill, it is already decided," she said with finality. "The new riding instructor will take over your lessons beginning tomorrow."

Stunned into silence, I sat there with a lump in my throat and a tear rolling down my face. Amy nudged my arm.

"I called all of your students and told them that you will no longer be teaching here. Maybe you can come back in the summer," she said coldly. Each staccato word out of her mouth crushed my heart, and I felt wounded under her verbal assault.

"Okay," I managed to squeak out.

With that, she hung up the phone, and I allowed all my emotions to empty out onto my pillow. I was devastated.

Teaching riding lessons was a dream that put my own riding abilities to the test. I arrived at the farm an hour before lessons started, and I skipped lunch so that I could squeeze every student into my day. I stayed late and helped feed the horses. I dressed professionally by wearing boots, britches, a vest, and riding jacket. The other instructors were always dressed unprofessionally. They wore shorts or cutoff jeans and sneakers—and were usually late.

Unlike the other instructors, I combed through every book that dealt with horseback riding, went to clinics, watched videos, and observed other instructors. I was determined to be the best. I became a certified riding instructor by passing rigorous tests, which few people can do.

Beth's conversation was something I never dreamed I would have to deal with. It hit me like a ton of bricks out of the blue. I was sick to my stomach with the realization that I had just been fired. I had never gotten fired in my whole life. Working hard, striving to be the best, and never disappointing anyone made me into an exemplary employee and the winner of the coveted award, Governor's Teacher of the Year in New Jersey.

Beth and I were not best friends, but good friends because of our mutual love of horses. I respected her, and she respected me. Or at least I thought so.

But I knew my firing wasn't about me being stressed out or not doing a good job. After staying at her house and experiencing the forces that were at work in her home, she was leery of me and our relationship was strained. Now we were both uncomfortable with each other.

Also, I knew her "secrets" that she kept from the outside world. Because she was well off financially, many people thought she had the ideal, perfect life. Much of it was a lie, and I was aware of how much this woman hurt. I witnessed her husband spinning the tires of his truck on the soft rain-soaked dirt so that he purposely got mud in her face. I knew the scared and frightened Beth. She was always looking for something better, never satisfied with anything—even this home or her state-of-the-art horse farm. She once shared with me that she was having clandestine meetings with ex-boyfriends. She was always searching for something to fill the void of her aching heart. Deep down, I think she knew that I had what she did not have. She had the money, but I had the peace and that prized possession—a relationship with the King of Kings, and that was priceless.

I tried to broach the subject with Beth about having a relationship with God, but she dismissed me and said that she already did. Like many people, she felt that attending church would help her on her journey toward finding that elusive relationship. I felt sorry for her. She was lost and slipping on a path that would only lead to destruction.

Again, I went to the Bible and prayed for direction. I had always heard that cliché, "If God closes a door, He will always open a window." Where was the window? I pondered this and tried not to sulk in my self-doubt and bitterness.

I slept heavily that night. No alarm going off at five in the morning meant I could sleep in and ride my horse instead of teaching. I felt a deep sadness creep in and spread across my heart, but I also felt slightly liberated, as if something better was going to happen.

The next day, I had a leisurely breakfast and went out to the barn where I kept my horse, and rode with a few people at the stable. It was fun to be in the company of my old friends. Then I went home to take a shower and get ready for a date.

When I got home, my answering machine was blinking with missed calls and several messages. The last message was left at 3:10 p.m. It was Beth. I had just missed the call.

"You have to work next Saturday," she said. "Call me as soon as you can."

The next message was from one of my adult students: "Jill, I had no idea you weren't going to be there today. I was so disappointed that I told Beth off. She said that you were stressed out and were taking time off until the summer. I told her that I was going to wait until you got back. The instructor they replaced you with is a real dip. She did not have a clue. Hey, call me if you can! I left without a lesson today, and I guess I'll have to wait until you come back."

Several other messages were similar. The students said that they didn't like the new instructor and were going to wait until I got back.

I got into the shower and was thinking things over when I heard the phone ringing again. I turned off the shower, wrapped myself in my fluffy cotton robe, and grabbed the phone. It was Beth.

"Uh, were you going to call me?" she asked sharply.

"I just got in, Beth, and I just got out of the shower," I said.

"Well, this isn't working. You need to teach next Saturday," she said.

There was so much loathing in her voice that it was almost palpable. It was as if she was blaming me for my students' reactions.

"Why, what happened?" I already knew the answer but felt I needed to hear it from her.

"Well, it seems your students don't want to take lessons with anyone else. Some of them even yelled at me. I am so disgusted with them. When they found out that you would not be coming back until the summer, they said that they would wait rather than ride with this wonderful new instructor, Kate, whom I hired. I don't want to lose your students, so you need to come back!" She was almost screaming.

Beth never wanted me to come back. She intended for me to be out of her life because I knew too much about her. She was vulnerable with me around. But my students were ruining her plans. *More important*, I thought, *God's plans could not be foiled.*

"I will come back the following weekend," I said. "I made plans to take my nephew to Lancaster next Saturday."

"Okay," she said and hung up.

My fate was sealed. I knew that Beth did not like anyone besides her being in control. But the fact was, she was not in control of my students, and this bothered her. I made up my mind at that moment I did not want to work at another farm except my very own.

I began to believe that "with God all things are possible," so I was going to take God at His word and believe that a single woman working as a teacher would be able to do the impossible—buy her own horse farm. No longer would I have to work at someone else's farm and suffer the humiliation of being fired.

Our relationship never healed, and there was a strain and uneasiness I always felt when I was around Beth. My days were numbered there, but the time at her farm taught me many valuable and priceless lessons.

First, I would forever be changed by my acceptance of Jesus Christ as my Savior. Second, I knew that being a riding instructor was a calling for which I was incredibly gifted. Third, I learned that my focus would not be on finding another farm where I could teach riding, but purchasing my own farm. Fourth, God had shown me that nothing was impossible with Him. All I had to do was believe and trust Him, and I could fulfill all my dreams and desires.

—∿—

Epilogue

"I love this home. We drive by it every day, and each day my wife implores me to stop and meet the owner. You see, we have a colonial home two blocks away, and she broke her hip falling down the stairs. Now she is scared, and we really need a ranch home that she will no longer have to walk down steps. I don't know if you would be interested in selling your home, but we would be interested in buying it."

They were an older couple, the woman with perfectly coiffed fifties-styled hair and the man with a full head of thick white hair and wearing a sports jacket. He explained that he was retired and his wife had been a homemaker. They had raised their children in this neighborhood and did not want to leave what they had known as home.

This little home I bought five years ago in Delaware represented sweat equity. What I could not afford to hire out, I did myself. Every inch of the deep-red oak had been painstakingly sanded by my hands. Each paneled wall had been pulled down by me, replaced with fresh drywall, and painted light, crisp colors. Shag carpet from the seventies had been pulled up and replaced with thick wool carpet from a wholesale warehouse in Philadelphia. It was here that I cemented my foundation in Christ by reading the Bible, journaling my experiences, and praising the Lord.

Also, it was here I had access to a private park that included horse trails, doggy parks for Amy, and hiking trails for me to walk or run every day. It was centrally located. Within ten miles of my home, I could be in Maryland or Pennsylvania. Shopping was great, the restaurants were even better, and it was surrounded by rolling hills.

As a single woman, it was a huge step in independence and responsibility. I learned more about myself living in this home than at any other time in my life. Realizing that I was capable of what I thought was impossible—transforming this broken and neglected home into a showplace, complete with gleaming hardwood floors and a now open-floor plan—gave me confidence that I could do anything I set my mind to accomplish.

My dream had always been to own a horse farm, and this first home was the stepping stone of confidence that let me know I could achieve seemingly impossible feats. Although I had been praying for this, I did not think it could materialize in the form of two people knocking on my door and offering what I thought was impossible.

Matthew 19:26 states, "With God all things are possible." This was becoming my own personal verse. I was realizing that God didn't work within ordinary parameters but in extraordinary ones. *How many people sell their homes when they aren't even up for sale?* I wondered. It was another confirmation that God was teaching me to expect the unexpected.

I promised to get back to them within a few days regarding my decision. That morning I took a long walk in the private park with my faithful Amy. One part of me was excited, the other part scared. Fearful of making a huge mistake both financially and physically, I weighed the decision like a deep-sea diver who wanted to make sure that he had enough oxygen.

As a born-again Christian, I had the ultimate guide in wisdom: God. I prayed every waking moment. I held onto the hope that God would give me the desires of my heart, even a heart that was scared.

Psalm 37:4 (ESV) became a palpable jacket that I put on each day: *Delight yourself in the LORD, and He will give you the desires of your heart.*

So, that October of 2001, I sold my house to the couple who promised to care for my home as well as I had. I made so much money off the sale of my house that I had enough money to purchase a farm. Within an hour of settlement, I drove to my church and handed the church pastor 10 percent of the final sale. We prayed together that God would lead me to a farm.

In the meantime, I had some healing in my relationship with my mother and moved back in with her and my dad. I searched diligently in four states—Delaware, New Jersey, Maryland, and Pennsylvania—for the perfect farm. I went to barns in disrepair, homes that were deplorable, and pastures overgrown with nettles and briars. I was becoming discouraged, and it seemed that though outwardly God was answering my prayers, inwardly I was seeing no results. I was losing hope.

One day in April, I climbed Thunder Hill in the Brandywine Valley, an area known to have been struck by lightning because of its elevation. I chose it because I could see for miles and I felt somewhat closer to God. In two short months, I would celebrate my fortieth birthday, which was my imaginary deadline to acquire the farm. If I did not buy a farm by then, I would give up this dream. Unfortunately, settlement on a farm usually takes longer than a standard home because of regulations and inspections. Each day that drew closer to June 3rd was like a stabbing pain that throbbed and stung about my impossible dream.

And then Martha, my realtor, left a message on my cell phone voice-mail.

"Jill, I found a place you may be interested in. Do you want to stop by and pick up the listing? I will leave it on my secretary's desk. Call me after you drive by to see if you want to go inside. See you!"

She was no longer driving out to these obscure farms with me. While visiting one farm, all the horses broke down the fence and ran after her. Running through the pastures in her perfectly manicured nails, silk business suit, and stiletto heels while screaming hysterically was not her idea of fun. And having a client like me, who would refuse to get out of the car after driving for hours to see what appeared on paper to be the perfect farm, only to find it horrific, was just too much. We came to an understanding that she would stay put, and I would explore the listings on my own.

I threw my school books into the car and drove off to Martha's office to pick up the listing. The home was listed as a modern farm house, and the picture was slightly blurry. I was not impressed, but on a whim, I decided to go. As I drove into southern New Jersey, the land began to change. There were large, expansive farms with picture-perfect fields filled with apple and peach trees. The roads curved and twisted over hills, forests, and open land. I was falling in love with the area with its grand old homes and large bank barns made of stone.

When I arrived, I noticed that the generous home had a wrap-around porch. There were two barns and automatic waterers for the horses. The land was flat with a stream in the back of the property, and I pictured myself sitting in the back writing and reading. I immediately picked up the phone and called Martha.

"Martha, can I see this home? I'm actually sitting in the front of it." I was growing excited.

"You like it?" she asked with a lift in her voice of incredulity. "Okay, I just need to make a few phone calls. Hang out in town, and I'll be in touch." She sounded confident.

"Martha, I love it. It's exactly as I pictured what my farm would look like," I said.

"Okay, stay near your phone."

"No problem. I look forward to getting inside."

I smiled with the thought of me getting what seemed totally improbable.

Martha arrived within an hour. As I walked into the home, I was struck by its magnificence. Hardwood floors and a gleaming staircase with a marble entryway spoke volumes about the former owner's care of the house. The master bedroom had a bathroom with a large Jacuzzi tub. It was so decadent that I almost started to cry.

"Well, what do you think?" Martha asked.

"Let's do it!" I almost screamed with excitement.

On May 31, 2002, I bought a beautiful horse farm that I named Raise Your Dreams, after my beloved horse. It was here that I learned volumes about God, His power, and most important, His promises full of hope. Within a year, I would be married to the most knowledgeable man about the Bible and one whom I admired deeply. We were married on the wrap-around porch, surrounded by friends and family.

Today, I have more land. The farm has grown with six horses, two dogs, twenty barn cats, and the best husband in the world. I have learned that "with God, all things are possible." His Word has permeated my soul, and I am foolish enough to believe that what He says is true.

And it is all true, every word and letter in the Bible. Every day, miracles abound at this little farm in southern New Jersey, where dreams are fulfilled and the biggest one was mine—to own a farm to teach special-needs children, to reach those who are lost, and to love the ones who need it the most.

Conclusion

—⁓—

I started writing this book more than twenty years ago. Writing was an outlet that allowed me the ability to process all that I was experiencing. I have left some experiences out that I felt would be too terrifying or emotional, but I've kept the integrity of the story—my story of how I came to know the King of Kings through an experience that was like no other.

As I wrote and re-wrote this book, editing and fine-tuning it, I prayed that God would write through me, telling you His story. His story is lived out in the lives of all believers, because with God all things are possible.

My life as I knew it was shattered and torn apart, but built up into a glorious testimony of what God Almighty can do—not what I can do.

Would you like to have a life that God can work through? Easy. Just ask Jesus to come into your life.

First, confess that you are a sinner and Jesus is the Son of God.

Second, ask Jesus to come into your heart and cleanse it.

Third, believe that Jesus is the Lord of Lords and King of Kings.

Next, live a life blessed by the only one who has the power to bless, Jesus Christ.

May your life be filled with His glorious presence!

Be blessed!

Afterword

⁓

On August 30, 2017, as this book was in the final stages of publishing, I was diagnosed with an aggressive form of cancer. Yesterday, before my port was put in to receive chemotherapy, the nurse asked the standard protocol procedure questions:

Name?

Date of Birth?

What surgery are you having?

I looked at the petite nurse before me and said, "I am having the destroyer put in. You know it as a port. It is my second line of defense."

The nurse asked, "What is your first line of defense?"

I said, "Well, let me tell you about Him . . ."

Meet the Author

Jill Dorsey Mansor is the owner of Raise Your Dreams Farm in Woodstown, New Jersey. Recently retired after thirty-three years of public high school teaching, she now is an adjunct instructor at a local university. She was awarded the New Jersey Governor's Teacher of the Year Award in 1994 and has developed and implemented many programs for special-needs children.

Jill has been featured on the Christian Broadcast Network TV program, *The 700 Club*. She has also been featured on the Philadelphia Eagles' Football TV Network. Numerous articles have been written about her farm and her work in the *South Jersey Times and Salem Sunbeam* and in the *Woodbury and West Deptford Life* magazine. Jill was also featured on the ARC Radio Network to discuss the equine therapy program she runs at her farm. In 2014, Raise Your Dreams Farm was selected as the "Best of Pilesgrove."

Jill is most passionate about telling her story of how her life and work were transformed by accepting Jesus Christ as her personal Savior. She is enthusiastic about her book and is in the process of writing several others.

Today Jill owns six horses, twenty barn cats, and two huge dogs, and lives at the farm of her dreams with her husband, Dan.

Order Info

—⁓—

Fighting for the Finish

is available from amazon.com, fruitbearer.com,
or wherever books are sold.
For autographed books or to schedule speaking engagements,
contact the author at
jmansor62raiseyourdreamsfarm@yahoo.com

Published by Fruitbearer Publishing, LLC
P.O. Box 777 • Georgetown, DE 19947
302.856.6649 • FAX 302.856.7742
fruitbearer.com • info@fruitbearer.com